STAND AT THE CROSS AND BE CHANGED

E. LONNIE MELASHENKO
AND JOHN THOMAS MCLARTY

Pacific Press Publishing Association
Nampa, Idaho
Oshawa, Ontario, Canada

Edited by Kenneth R. Wade
Cover and inside design by Michelle C. Petz

Copyright ©1997 by
Pacific Press Publishing Association
Printed in the United States
All Rights Reserved

Melashenko, E. Lonnie.
    Stand at the Cross and be changed / E. Lonnie
Melashenko and John Thomas McLarty.
        p.   cm.
    ISBN 0-8163-1384-9 (alk. paper)
    1. Jesus Christ—Crucifixion—Sermons. 2. Seventh-
day Adventists—Sermons. 3. Sermons, American.
I. McLarty, John, 1952- II. Title.
BT450.M45 1997
232.96—dc21   96-48568
                                                     CIP

97 98 99 00 01 • 5 4 3 2 1

TABLE OF CONTENTS

Preface 5

Introduction 9

Glossary and Cast of Characters 17

1. The Divine Plot: Simon of Cyrene 21

2. Just Doing a Job: The Soldiers 31

3. Father, Forgive Them 41

4. Most Favored Woman: Mary, Jesus' Mother 49

5. Woman, There Is Your Son 59

6. He Sinned His Way to God: The Repentant Thief 67

7. Paradise Guaranteed 75

8. A Great Pharisee: Nicodemus 83

9. Abandoned! My God, Why Have You Forsaken Me? 97

10. Mary Magdalene 105

11. I'm Thirsty! 115

12. Retraining the Thunder: John, Part One 123

13. First Place: John, Part Two 131

14. It Is Finished! 137

15. The Loser: Caiaphas 143

16. Into Your Hands 153

PREFACE

This book had its beginning in a series of sermons I preached while pastoring in Paradise. (Paradise, California, that is.) The church in Paradise had experienced severe conflict and even schism. It seemed to me that the best medicine for my church would be a fresh look at Jesus Christ, especially at His sacrifice on the cross.

Now, as director/speaker of the international radio broadcast, *The Voice of Prophecy*, I am more convinced than ever that a clear vision of Jesus is the most hopeful remedy not only for fragmenting congregations, but the disintegrating global community as well. Conflicts between generations, races, ethnic groups, economic classes, nations, and the sexes have at their root memories—real and imagined—of past injustice and fear of future harm. But the power and love of Jesus can counteract these poisonous animosities and neutralize the most potent hatreds; His grace can bring forgiveness into the most hostile relationships.

Jesus is our only hope. The good news is that He is *sufficient* hope.

God has created in our hearts a hunger to know Him. We

find that hunger most fully satisfied in coming to know Jesus Christ. As we come to know Jesus, He gives us peace here and now and the assurance of eternal life. Jesus said, " And I, if I am lifted up from the earth, will draw all peoples to Myself " (John 12:32, NKJV). One of the ways we can increase the power of Jesus' attraction in our lives is to deliberately focus our minds on the events, the people, and words connected with His crucifixion.

The crucifixion of Jesus has been an inexhaustible spring of inspiration not only for preachers, but for painters, writers, sculptors, musicians, poets, and the rest of us as we experience the joys and hardships common to humanity.

More books have been written on the life and death of Jesus Christ than have been written about any other person. His influence has left its conspicuous mark in the music and art of Western culture. Who can resist the pathos of the "Saint Matthew Passion" by Bach, the "Seven Last Words" by Dubois, or the Easter portion of Handel's "Messiah"? Michelangelo's Pietà, Salvador Dali's "Crucifixion," and the anonymously carved crucifixes of primitive societies all speak of the grip on human imagination held by Jesus, the divine Son of God, who created earth and its residents and then allowed His own creation to murder Him.

One of the pleasures of preparing the sermons that led to this book was reading what others had written about Jesus. The most obvious source is the New Testament, especially the little books titled Matthew, Mark, Luke, and John. It is my hope that this book will cause the reader to want to read again the story of Jesus as told by these four authors.

Several books by modern authors were very helpful. One that I have read several times, and return to often for inspiration, is *The Desire of Ages*, by Ellen G. White. There is no finer comprehensive presentation of the life of Christ.

Another book every Christian should have the opportunity to read is the classic by Jim Bishop, *The Day Christ Died.* In his book, *When God Met Men,* Arthur L. Bietz focuses on people who knew Jesus personally. His book provided many practical insights. Useful also was Fulton J. Sheen's book, *Characters of the Passion.*

Finally, I must mention *These Watched Him Die* by Leslie Hardinge. I thank him for helping me, through his preaching and writing, to join those who watched Christ die, and to see through their eyes the greatest event in human history.

For the newcomer to the world of Bibles: You will note that quotations from the Bible are followed by abbreviations. These indicate various translations of the Bible. They are:

KJV—King James Version
NKJV—New King James Version
NEB—New English Bible
TEV—Today's English Version
NIV—New International Version

Quotations marked Paraphrase are paraphrases based primarily on the five English translations mentioned above. Almost always they are combinations of two or more of these translations.

The chapters in this book fall into two distinct groups. One set of chapters profiles people who were at the cross. In these chapters we look at what happened on Golgotha through their eyes. The other set of chapters focuses on what Jesus said while He was hanging on the cross. The two sets are intermixed.

This book would never have been written without Mrs. Violet Fleming, who transcribed over two hundred pages of the original sermon tapes. I cannot thank her enough. My thanks also to John McLarty, my friend and colleague at The

Voice of Prophecy, for shaping the sermons into a book. There is much of him in these pages.

The story of Jesus is never told . . . once for all. Every generation must "tell it again." That is what preaching is about. That is what this book is about.

Literature, music, art, scholarship, the history of the Christian church—all testify that something momentous happened when Jesus of Nazareth climbed Golgotha and hung on a cross. Throughout the last two thousand years, believers have found courage and hope in the words and actions of Jesus on that last day of His life.

All of us long for greater power to do right. Many of us need help overcoming the distrust of God that has been built into us by our personal histories. We want to know God. A clear vision of Jesus on the cross will kindle in us admiration, devotion, and joy. It will create in us tranquil confidence in His compassion. It will make us new people. May this book help the reader see what really happened when Jesus allowed Himself to be crucified. May it help the last words of Jesus have the maximum impact in your life.

Introduction:
The Preacher,
the Place, the Audience

The sermon was about to begin. The congregation had gathered, their attention riveted on the preacher. Even angels grew tense with expectancy in the wait. Mere curiosity and the contagious excitement of a crowd accounted for some of the audience. Love brought some. Hatred others. The eyes of some in the crowd burned from hours of crying for the man whose sermons and whose touch had restored their dignity and given meaning to their lives. Others stood, arms folded, coolly savoring their victory over a troublesome dissident.

Jesus of Nazareth had preached from all kinds of pulpits—from a boat on Lake Galilee, from His couch while reclining at dinner in the homes of pariahs, and in the mansions of Brahmins. He had preached on hillsides and in synagogues in Galilee. In Jerusalem, crowds had hung on His words in the temple courtyard. And He had interrupted His words with tears as He stood on Mount Olivet overlooking Jerusalem—weeping for His city and its heartbreaking future.

Now in preparation for His last sermon, Jesus, Immanuel, Almighty-God-in-the-Flesh* stretched out His arms on the cross. From that dramatic pulpit, hands spread-eagled, He faced

9

the Holy City for the last time. Delivered His final sermon.

Phoenicians invented crucifixion. It was the final stage in their search for the perfect execution. Death by spear, boiling in oil, impalement, drowning, asphyxiation, strangulation, burning—all had been tried. But they lacked the necessary shame, and they were too quick. Crucifixion was ideal. It was shameful. The victims were stripped naked and hung up for everyone to see. Often they were flogged before being crucified. On the cross flies, gnats, and ants joined the humans in tormenting the crucified. Crucifixion was wonderfully slow; death did not bring relief too quickly. Vultures and other carrion feeders lingered nearby, waiting.

The Romans perfected the Phoenician invention. Once, after the collapse of a rebellion led by Spartacus the slave, they crucified 6,000 men in a single day, planting their crosses along a hundred miles of road from Capua to Rome.

When Jesus' turn to be crucified came on Friday afternoon, He was just another cipher in an unending routine for His executioners. They threw Him down; the soldier with the hammer planted his knee on Jesus' forearm, probing with his finger to find the soft, hollow spaces between the bones.

The nails were five inches long. A few powerful strokes with the hammer sank them into the wood. The preacher was fixed to his pulpit. The soldiers, grunting, hoisted pulpit and preacher and rammed the upright into the prepared hole.

Hecklers immediately targeted the preacher. Crucifixions were cheap fun for the lowlifes of Jerusalem. The rulers had let it out on the street that rowdies would be welcome. So they were there, jeering, jesting, jostling for the best view of the three men nailed up against the sky. To these crude ruffians, the three men on crosses were just three more crooks getting what they had coming, suckers who had pushed their luck too far. Too bad.

But some in the mob had known the Man on the middle cross. They had eaten bread and fish served by His disciples; they had been astounded by His miracles, moved by His preaching. Still they joined the scorn and mockery. Jesus had put on a good show while it lasted, but His present situation was proof enough that He was an impostor. And to think they'd almost believed Him! How relieved they were this afternoon that they hadn't been taken in.

Snatches of sermons they had heard in synagogues and on mountainsides came back to them. And these they twisted and hurled in His face. "You said you could build the temple in three days. Won't it be a little hard to do that with your arms nailed down? What kind of carpenter are you anyway?"

"You claimed you were older than Father Abraham. Well, you sure look old now, old enough to die! But we're sure you're still young enough to run away if you'd work just one more miracle. You walked on water. Why can't you climb down from that cross?"

After each crude joke, guffaws, snorts, and howls swept through the crowd. Men tried to best each other with their ribaldry; those who couldn't compete with wit bellowed the loudest with laughter. They had no idea they were attacking God. They were merely enjoying laughs with the gang at the expense of some poor fool on a cross. There was no way this haggard Preacher could be Messiah. A charlatan? Maybe. Or a visionary whose imagination had overwhelmed his good sense? A religious fanatic, a megalomaniac? Perhaps. But Messiah, Saviour of humanity, Immanuel? Not a chance.

But even in their mockery they conceded His power: "Hey, miracle man, where's your power now? People lame from the day they were born jumped around like frogs after you got through with them. Why don't you jump down from the cross? We've even heard that you raised the dead. What's the matter with you now? Have you lost your powers? Come on down. One more miracle's all you need!"

The Romans in the audience, the centurion and his soldiers, scarcely heard the crowd. They were doing their job, and they were done with the hard part. They could relax and let nature take its course.

They tossed dice for their shares of the prisoners' clothes. They talked about women and home and parties. They cared nothing for the Preacher. They knew nothing of Him.

Not until the sky went black and the ground shook like a rag in a terrier's mouth—not until then—did they take special notice of the Preacher.

The leaders of the nation-church huddled in a small cluster in the middle of the rabble. Caiaphas, the high priest; his father-in-law, Annas, high priest emeritus; and other dignitaries were nearly limp with relief at how easily they had won. Pilate had not given them too much difficulty. There had been no public uprising in support of the carpenter-turned-preacher. Orthodoxy, the priesthood, the glory of the temple were all more secure now because of their decisive action in arresting this innovator from Galilee.

Death was always a pity. But as Caiaphas had said, it was better that one man should die than for the whole nation to perish. Their job wasn't easy, but it had to be done.

As they recovered from their fear that even at the last moment the Preacher might surprise them, might escape them, they lost their reserve. The mob they had created seduced them. They were drawn into taunting the Preacher. "He trusted in God; let God deliver him now, if he'll have him. After all, he did say, 'I am the Son of God.' Come on down now, Mr. Jesus," they snorted, "and we'll be convinced. We'll all become believers."

It never entered the minds of these august clergy that the

energy of the crowd they had gathered was fueled by a choir of evil angels. Little did they dream that their own chants of derision reflected the gloating of the evil one.

The Preacher was a dangerous man. He had diverted thousands of people from concern for historic theology. He challenged Jewish self-confidence and the concern for behavioral standards so valued by Jewish conservatives. He gave people a new, heart-warming picture of a caring God. He taught them to value compassion and integrity more than ideological and traditional correctness. He had made the priesthood look bad. But He did not look so good Himself now—bloody, naked, emaciated. To the senior clergy gathered on Golgotha, Jesus' words from the cross meant nothing. The sermon announcement tacked to the wood above His head, "This is Jesus of Nazareth, the King of the Jews," annoyed them, but it said nothing to their consciences.

Jesus had company in His agony that afternoon—two thieves. All three were treated like any other criminals by professional executioners. They were stripped and nailed to their crosses. All three suffered terribly from the agonies of thirst, shame, and the unspeakable pain that began in their arms and feet and then spread to their chests and viscera. The thieves cursed the soldiers, God, life, and their pain. They picked up the taunts of the crowd against the Preacher. "Hey, you. If you're *really* the Messiah, get us out of here. Save yourself and take us along with you."

It was a while before either thief was ready to listen.

Neither thief had volunteered for his place in Jesus' entourage that afternoon. They were not given the privilege of sharing the platform with Jesus as a reward for their good lives. But for one of them, the punishment of his sin was transformed into a stupendous benefit by words from the dying Preacher.

Not every human in the audience scorned the Preacher. Mary of Bethany crouched at the foot of the pulpit. Years before, so tradition has it, Mary of Bethany had become Mary of Magdala, her innocence and gentle goodness given away or stolen, who could tell. But now nothing could keep her from Jesus—not Roman soldiers nor an abusive mob nor cowering friends. She pushed her way through to the foot of His cross. She loved Him.

Just a few days earlier, she had sneaked into a dinner party and poured a whole bottle of expensive perfume on Him. Poured it gladly and cried and kissed His feet. She had been broken when Jesus found her, a wretched specter, a used car, damaged merchandise, consigned by proper folk to the human junk heap. Jesus had rescued her. He had made her a woman again. He had given her worth, love, hope, life. She was His. She was there, ready for the Preacher's last sermon.

Another Mary was there, Jesus' mother, Mary of Nazareth. She, too, was doggedly loyal. She could not understand what was happening. She had hoped Jesus would be the salvation of Israel. She remembered the dreams and visits by angels. She hadn't just imagined them. And the shepherds' report and the visit by the Magi were real beyond question. Jesus' destiny had seemed so clear. She had not understood the dark words of Simeon, whispered at the temple thirty some-odd years ago when she and Joseph had presented their Baby: "A sword shall pierce your own soul also." She did not understand then, did not understand now. But no matter, Jesus was her Son. She sobbed brokenly beside His pulpit.

John was there, helpless, steeling himself against the devastation of his life. For three years he had worked for this Man, listening to His sermons, observing His incredible powers, learning the depth of His goodness. Jesus had become his best friend, with the words "best" and "friend" pushed to the limit of their meaning.

Now, with Jesus dying, John had nothing left to live for, except for the Marys. He had to be strong for them. This ending made no sense, but somehow for their sake, he had to be strong. Jesus would want it that way.

Others of the Twelve were there too. Ashamed of their cowardice on Thursday night. Scared. Trying to console the many women who had followed Jesus all the way from Galilee, even thought they themselves had no answers, no hope. They all had loved this Preacher, not purely, not unflaggingly, but truly. Who could not?

These men hated the priests and the mob shouting at their Leader. They wished they could do something. It was good that the women were there. At least, the disciples could act like men by holding their sobbing sisters.

The anger of Jesus' friends was shared by heavenly angels who stood unseen among them. Only the stern order of God restrained them from blasting the blaspheming crowd around the cross. The angels would have needed but a split second to snatch out the nails and lift Jesus away from His tormentors. But orders were orders. So the angels agonized with Jesus' earthly friends, wishing they could hold them all and share their grief.

There were people in the audience that day apparently quite by happenstance, caught up in the crowd as it swept out of the city. But as the movement stopped at the top of the hill and the crowd began to separate into groups of friends and enemies, Romans and Jews, rulers and rabble, these chance participants in the drama were compelled to choose their places. Would they laugh or weep, leave or stare with cold fascination? The group they lingered in shaped their sympathies. Their reaction to the Preacher became indistinguishable from their choice of where to stand.

The drama on Golgotha that Friday afternoon was a microcosm of all human history. It was the overture for the final judgment, presenting in brief the themes that will be fully developed when God summons the world to account. On Golgotha, as in every age, the most crucial questions concerned Jesus: What do you think of Jesus? What will you do with Him? Where will you stand?

Any sermon consists of more than just words; it includes the influence of the preacher's character and experience. So with Jesus. Each listener's acquaintance with Jesus powerfully shaped the impact of His words. So with us. Our relationship with Him colors what we hear.

Each listener hears something different in a sermon. In this book we will try to hear what the different people heard from the crucified Jesus. We want to hear everything Jesus said in His sermon, the whole truth, every possible nuance.

All mankind was gathered at the cross. Enemies of Jesus, friends, hangers-on, the curious, the passers-by, people just doing a job. Scripture-quoting, Bible-believing, devout church leaders. Hypocrites, harlots, and their customers. Hardened men of the world whose language was nonstop vulgarity. Almost-believers, had-been believers, never-would-be believers, believers. They are us. Their story is our story. Their Preacher speaks to us. Let's stand and listen to Him and to those who heard Him speak.

* A glossary of terms that may be unfamiliar, and a cast of characters, is provided on page 17.

Glossary and Cast of Characters

We hope that many will read this book who are just discovering the Bible. If you are one of these new acquaintances, the following glossary and cast of characters may help you understand more readily this story of Jesus.

Almighty-God-in-the-Flesh
A name for Jesus that highlights the fact that He was both truly God and truly human.

Centurion
A Roman army officer comparable to a corporal or sergeant.

Christ-killers
Every human being. The term captures the reality that each human, as a sinner, has contributed directly to the cause of Jesus' death.

Daniel
An Old Testament prophet who wrote amazingly detailed predictions about the Messiah.

Disciple
1. A member of the group of twelve men Jesus appointed as His closest associates. 2. Anyone identified as a follower of Jesus.

17

Dysmas
Legendary name of the thief who accepted Jesus. The name does not appear in the Bible.

Elijah
An Old Testament prophet whose ministry was highly confrontational. He was seen variously as symbolic of a forerunner of the Messiah or of the Messiah Himself.

Elisha
Elijah's successor. His ministry as a prophet was much less confrontational than Elijah's. Elisha established schools and acted as pastor to the nation. He worked many remarkable miracles.

Golgotha
The hill outside Jerusalem where crucifixions were performed.

Immanuel
A Hebrew name for Jesus, which means literally "God with us" (Matthew 1:23).

Isaiah
An ancient prophet whose writings contain some of the most explicit descriptions of the ministry of the Messiah.

Jeremiah
An Old Testament prophet.

John
One of the twelve disciples. Author of five books in the New Testament. Understood to be "the disciple whom Jesus loved" mentioned in the Gospel of John.

John the Baptist
A fiery preacher who stirred the Jewish nation by his call for Jews to be baptized (immersed in the Jordan River) as a sign of their renunciation of sin and acceptance of God's mercy. He explicitly predicted the imminent appearance of the Messiah. Jesus' first disciples came from among the disciples of John the Baptist.

Joseph (of Nazareth)
The husband of Mary, the stepfather of Jesus, probably the father of Jesus' brothers.

Joseph of Arimathea

A member of the Sanhedrin who hid his sympathies for Jesus out of fear of social and political repercussions. He came forward at Jesus' death to provide a decent burial.

Longinus

Traditional name of the centurion who superintended Jesus' crucifixion. The name is not in the Bible.

Magi

Wealthy visitors to the infant Jesus, probably aristocrats from Persia who were familiar with the Jewish Scriptures and with Jewish expectancy of a Messiah.

Mary (of Nazareth)

The mother of Jesus, probably stepmother to Jesus' brothers.

Mary of Magdala, or Mary Magdalene

A woman delivered by Jesus from demon possession. Traditionally identified with Mary of Bethany, sister of Martha and Lazarus, and with the "sinful woman" mentioned in Luke 7:36-50.

Messiah

Hebrew for "the anointed one." The divine personage who would end history by establishing an eternal kingdom characterized by universal justice and morality.

Old Testament

The modern name for the first two-thirds of the Bible. It was written by Jewish authors over a thousand-year period, approximately from 1450 B.C. to 425 B.C. It was the Bible in Jesus' day.

New Testament

The modern name for the last one-third of the Bible, written during the sixty years after the death and resurrection of Jesus.

Nicodemus

The foremost conservative scholar of his day. He was wealthy and a member of the Sanhedrin. He was impressed with Jesus early on but tried to mask his sympathies until the day of the crucifixion.

Passover

The annual Jewish festival celebrating God's intervention to rescue Israel from Egyptian slavery in the days of Moses. Jews came to Jerusalem from all over the Mediterranean world to keep this feast.

Pentecost

An annual Jewish festival occurring fifty days after Passover. It was on this feast day fifty days after the crucifixion that the Holy Spirit came on the believers in a mighty way, accompanied with the outward sign of flames of fire above each believer's head. This triggered the beginning of the missionary work of the church.

Procurator

The administrator of the province of Judea under Roman occupation. Pilate was procurator at the time of Jesus' crucifixion.

Pharisees

A Jewish sect and political party that emphasized separation from the world in order to maintain personal righteousness. They had high regard for the authority of the Sacred Scriptures (the Old Testament). They believed in angels, the resurrection of the dead, and strict adherence to traditional rules regarding Sabbath keeping and other areas of life. They enjoyed the respect of a large portion of the common people.

Sadducees

A Jewish sect and political party, comprised mostly of the aristocracy. They balanced their lack of popular support with the power of wealth. They accepted only the first five books of the Old Testament as authoritative, denied certainty concerning angels and the resurrection, and were more relaxed in regard to the details of ritual obligations.

Samaritans

Natives of Samaria, a region between Judea and Galilee. Their religion included elements of several religions and included major elements of Judaism. They were disliked by the Jews for religious and racial reasons.

Sanhedrin

The council based in Jerusalem that combined legislative, judicial, and executive functions for Judea. Even under Roman occupation it exercised considerable power. It was also the supreme religious body for Jews the world over.

The Twelve

A title referring to the disciples, the twelve men Jesus appointed as His closest associates.

THE DIVINE PLOT:
SIMON OF CYRENE

> For to you it has been granted on behalf of Christ,
> not only to believe in Him, but also to suffer for His
> sake (Philippians 1:29 NKJV).

> God never leads His children otherwise than they
> would choose to be led, if they could see the end from
> the beginning, and discern the glory of the purpose
> which they are fulfilling. . . . Of all the gifts that Heaven
> can bestow upon men, fellowship with Christ in His
> sufferings is the most weighty trust and the highest
> honor (*The Desire of Ages*, 224, 225).

You have to believe a conspiracy theory of cosmic propor-
tions to make sense of Simon's story. The same is true of our
own stories. Simon believed. Perhaps, after you have heard his
story, you will too.

Under the midday sun, Simon walked in a river of pilgrims
on one of the approaches to Jerusalem. It was the eve of Passover. Looking around, Simon saw hair styles and beards, head-
gear and sandals, that spoke of a hundred different cultures.

He saw people from Gaul and Italy, from Cappadocia and Persia, from India and, perhaps, even from as far east as China. He could hear all kinds of strange languages in the babble of the crowd.

The traffic slowed as they neared the gate. Gazing up at the rough limestone blocks of the wall and the massive timbers of the gate, Simon choked with emotion. In all the miles since leaving his home town, Cyrene, in North Africa, nothing had stirred him like this. The Holy City, Mt. Zion, God's official earthly residence!

Tonight he would celebrate Passover in Jerusalem! He'd eat the bitter herbs and lamb. He'd recite the story of Israel's deliverance from Egypt. With others he would share in the annual rekindling of the ancient hope that God would send the Messiah to subjugate Israel's enemies and propel Jerusalem to unassailable world dominance. God would compel the senate and Caesar to bow to Jerusalem's sovereignty. Priests in the thousands of heathen temples scattered across the Roman Empire would recognize Jerusalem's temple as the only seat of true worship.

Simon had talked and believed these things since childhood. But the celebration tonight in Jerusalem would be the ultimate experience in his lifelong pursuit of the Almighty.

Finally, Simon made it through the bottleneck at the gate, but immediately he was slowed again. But what did he care? He was in Jerusalem! He stared, smelled, listened, oblivious to the jostling of the crowd, trying to fix the moment indelibly in his mind.

But this rapture was interrupted by shouts up ahead. People began squeezing themselves into the merchants' stalls that lined the crowded street. Craning his neck, Simon spotted the reason. Roman soldiers were opening a path through the traffic. Behind them walked three convicts, flanked and followed by more soldiers.

The procession was dogged by a mob of hecklers whose verbal venom stood Simon's hair on end.

Just as the vanguard of soldiers was almost abreast of Simon, a gasp ran through the crowd. One of the prisoners had fallen. Simon stood on tiptoe to see. The middle convict was down on His knees, His face in the dirt, a cross astride His back and tied to his wrists.

"Wha'd they do to that man?" Simon gasped. The prisoner's clothes were dark with blood. His hair was matted with dried blood. A guard was shouting at Him.

"On your feet, scum. Up. Let's go."

It was no use. The wood was not that heavy, but the prisoner could hardly walk, and the extra weight of the cross was simply too much.

When Jesus fell, women in the crowd began wailing and sobbing, but Simon, horrified, scarcely heard them.

"Can't they see He's done for?" he muttered to no one in particular. "Why do they beat a dead horse?" He watched the soldiers snatch at the ropes that fastened the crossbar to Jesus' wrists.

Simon was still staring at the fallen convict when a soldier grabbed him. He recoiled, twisted . . . and looked down at the point of a sword. "Hey, big man, get over here." The soldier hustled him into the center of the mob. Pointing at the cross lying on the stones beside Jesus, he ordered, "Pick it up!"

"Hey, what d'ya mean? I'm not from around here. You can't make me do this!"

"Pick it up!" roared the soldier. "Pick it up, or we'll nail it to you!"

Simon could hear snickers in the crowd. "What a rube!" somebody laughed. "That'll teach a pilgrim to open his mouth."

Simon was furious and bewildered. He had saved for years

for this trip. Now here he was on Friday afternoon, Passover eve, being forced to carry the cross of a man accused of treason and sedition! *Why are they picking on me?* Simon wondered. He didn't realize that his dark skin marked him as a foreigner and made him a prime candidate for impressment as a cross carrier.

In contemporary Western society, there is no parallel to the shame of crucifixion. The cross itself bore the curse of God. No citizen of Jerusalem could have been persuaded, without dire threats, to touch it. If the soldiers had attempted to draft a local for the job, they would have risked a riot.

The soldiers would not carry it. No decent officer would have required one of his own men to shoulder the symbol of execration.

We simply cannot comprehend the humiliation Simon felt as the soldier forced him into the center of that crowd. The disgrace was much more profound, more intense than any other embarrassment. The soldier had summoned him to a bottomless, black pit of horror and loathing. In addition to the public shame Simon was experiencing, the close contact with Roman soldiers and convicts would disqualify Simon from participating in this evening's and tomorrow's ceremonies, the high point of the Passover celebration. He'd be excluded from the congregation of God's people on what was supposed to be the most tremendous day of his life.

What terrible luck! The slightest alteration of his day . . . If he had left the inn this morning five minutes earlier, if he hadn't stopped at that well in the last village on his way into Jerusalem . . .

Simon stooped, picked up the timber, and hoisted it to his shoulder. A guard dragged the convict to His feet, and the procession prepared to move on again. But the convict raised His hand and with that simple movement took control. Simon was stunned. What secret power was this wasted convict hiding?

Turning to the wailing women, Jesus spoke quietly, but with arresting force, "Daughters of Jerusalem, do not weep for Me. Weep for yourselves and for your children. Hard times are coming to our beloved city—times so bad that mothers will wish they were childless spinsters. They will wish themselves dead.

"Dear women, if the good die young and cruelly now, now in the summertime of God's favor, imagine what will be true in the winter of His indignation.

"Do not weep for me. Weep for the suffering that will ruin our city when the time for choosing is over."

Jesus nodded to the soldier, and they started forward. Simon, massive and erect, stared ahead unseeing, masking the cringing and rage in his soul as he walked along beside the battered prophet. One of the soldiers sniggered: "We have a real king with us today. He even has a courtier to carry His stuff."

Jesus' words to the women still gripped Simon's attention. Before Jesus had spoken, Simon's mind had been completely filled with outrage at the injustice. Imagine, shanghaied by Roman thugs on Passover eve! As a devout Jew, he believed God controlled everything. God had done this to him, and it wasn't right. Simon had served God all his life—for this? Then Jesus had stopped the macabre parade with a gesture of His hand and quieted the wailing women with steel and velvet words about them and their city.

Simon was astonished. This Convict could hardly walk. He was on His way to His crucifixion! Yet, He spoke to these sobbing women with the dignity and compassion of a good king consoling His subjects for some grief in their hard scrabble lives. Who was this Man who cared more about the tears of these unknown women than about His own bloodied back and imminent crucifixion?

The abuse from the mob did not stop. The tears of the women and the veiled majesty of the Prisoner and His pain meant nothing to them. They were like sharks frenzied by the scent of blood. But as Simon walked, puzzling over the mysterious power and words of this Man, he discovered within himself a mysterious elation competing with his indignation. He held his head higher. He marched deliberately at the side of the Prisoner instead of slinking. His bold posture was no longer a facade. Whoever this Prisoner was, something inside Simon told him it was an honor to march with Him.

By the time Jesus was being paraded out of downtown Jerusalem toward Golgotha, Satan must have realized that when Jesus died on the cross, he, Satan, would suffer irreparable damage. He wanted to stop the juggernaut he had launched. He did not want Jesus to hang on Golgotha. When Jesus fell under His cross, Satan exulted; he had put off the final showdown. When Simon picked up the timber, however, Jesus' victory was assured. Simon did not know it yet, but Jesus was sharing His triumph. He and Simon climbed to the summit together.

One of the richest forms of intimacy, especially among men, is doing something together—fixing a car or coaching a team, working together on the finance committee at church or going on a mission trip, climbing mountains or going to war together. The most intense friendships develop between humans who have endured tough times together. Simon would never share richer, deeper fellowship with God than when he helped God the Son make the summit of Golgotha with His cross.

The soldier who grabbed Simon out of the crowd meant to do him no favor. But in reality by drafting Simon to carry that cross, he was calling him to act as prime minister in the kingdom of heaven. None of Jesus' disciples were available to help. Angels were disallowed from taking the job. Jesus, King of the Jews, King of the universe, needed a man to help Him accomplish the salvation of the world. Simon was His choice.

Naturally, Simon had no idea, at first, that this odious detour was the supreme honor of his life. How could he have known that carrying a Convict's cross would mean walking side-by-side with God? To create the opportunity of eternal life for all humanity, Jesus needed to get to Golgotha with His cross. On that Friday afternoon, He did not have the physical strength to do it. Simon's "bad luck" was, in fact, the privilege of helping Jesus save the world.

Jesus had once said, "If someone wishes to walk with Me, if someone wants to be My disciple, he must take up his cross and follow Me." There is no such thing as painless, effortless discipleship. But buried in the pain and effort is a treasury of joy.

Friday afternoon, surrounded by a jeering rabble, carrying a symbol of shame, Simon learned the truth of Jesus' words. That day's shame and ill fortune was his initiation into the joy of fellowship with Jesus. In time, he came to see that the cost of discipleship was itself part of the reward.

Simon's story speaks to us.

The pain in your life may feel like a curse; it may actually be a camouflage for God's presence. The birth of a retarded or deformed child can break your heart and rearrange your life. But it is not the curse of God. It may, in fact, be His richest blessing.

Before a child is born, parents dream. Their baby will be the most beautiful, the brightest, the sweetest ever born. Then comes the birth, and the parents confront the mind-numbing fact that their baby is retarded. The prognosis is twenty or thirty years of strenuous care before a premature death.

What a blasting of dreams! These parents hear the truth described in the cold facts of epidemiology—a certain number of every hundred thousand are born with defects just like your child's. But you wonder if perhaps God is punishing you for some blunder. Maybe He is repaying you for some offense against heaven. Or maybe God is just irritable, and you happened to be in the wrong place at the wrong time and caught His ire.

The good news, the sermon, in the story of Simon is that God is not mad at you. God is not punishing you. God *is responsible* at least to the extent that He allowed it to happen. He could have prevented it, but He didn't. So you can live with this confidence: in this suffering He can create an occasion for you and Him to walk together.

This applies to every difficulty: being abandoned to raise a disabled child all on your own, losing all your assets through business reverses or fraud, discovering you have a degenerative disease, finding yourself in a difficult marriage. God is able to transform every one of these disasters into occasions of camaraderie with Him.

Jesus did not leave Simon to carry the cross alone. Jesus kept company with Simon until he threw down the timber on Golgotha. Jesus will walk with the parents of a retarded or deformed or rebellious child until they can lay the burden down. Jesus did not allow Simon to be nailed to the cross he carried. And He will not allow you to be crucified on the cross in your life either.

If you are a mother whose husband has left you to rear the children alone, it may seem that God Himself has abandoned you. But God has not plotted against you. Your husband may be the personification of devilish self-centeredness. You may have made grave mistakes yourself that contributed to the difficulty of your situation. But the story of Simon reveals that in spite of these very real wrongdoings, your suffering can be turned by God into part of His plot to bring you into His presence.

If you are a pastor or pastor's wife serving in a difficult parish, you may wonder if you have missed your calling. Maybe God did not call you to the pastorate, or maybe He did not call you to this particular church. Conflict saps your strength and upsets your family. You wonder, *how can I possibly be in God's will if my life is so miserable?* The story of Simon demonstrates that sometimes what feels like bad luck or malicious politics or divine punishment is actually a disguised walk with Jesus.

Simon had almost no choice about whether or not to carry the cross. Similarly, there are some circumstances in which we apparently have little choice. We cannot ensure that all our children will be above average. We cannot make our spouses faithful and gentle and good. We cannot control the economy or even, ultimately, our own health. We may walk, at times, the via dolorosa—the way of sadness.

God could easily have arranged for Simon to miss the encounter with the soldiers. And God could have arranged our lives differently, changing our opportunities, overruling our choices. But He has not. But neither has He coldly left us to fate. Instead, God acts as the great conspirator. He works within the stream of events—good choices, bad choices, happenstances, and even the scheming and anger of foolish men—to bring us to Himself. For those who will allow Him access to their inner being, He uses everything for their ultimate good.

In the New Testament there is evidence that Simon and his family became Christians. If that is so, then what had seemed at the time to be the greatest disappointment of Simon's life became in later years the event in his life most treasured.

We can be sure that in his family for generations, the central story, the tale that gave them the greatest sense of family pride, was Grandpa Simon's afternoon on the via dolorosa carrying the cross for the Son of God—at the time, his bitterest disappointment; in reality, his greatest glory.

GOD MOVES IN A MYSTERIOUS WAY

God moves in a mysterious way
His wonders to perform;
He plants His footsteps in the sea,
And rides upon the storm.

Ye fearful saints, fresh courage take;
The clouds ye so much dread
Are big with mercy, and shall break
In blessings on your head.

Judge not the Lord by feeble sense,
But trust Him for His grace;
Behind a frowning providence
He hides a smiling face.

His purposes will ripen fast,
Unfolding every hour;
The bud may have a bitter taste,
But sweet will be the flower.
                    —William Cowper (1731-1800)

Just Doing a Job:
The Soldiers

For dogs have surrounded Me;
The assembly of the wicked has enclosed Me.
They pierced My hands and My feet;
I can count all My bones.
They look and stare at Me.
They divide My garments among them,
And for My clothing they cast lots
(Psalm 22:16-18, NKJV).

They had their orders. Jesus of Nazareth was to be crucified along with a couple of thieves already on death row. The soldiers slipped easily into the routine. They prepared the placards to be paraded before each prisoner announcing his crime. The uprights for the crosses were already at the Place of the Skull. From a storeroom they fetched the ropes and the timbers that would be used as the horizontal members of the crosses. They placed the heavy crossbars across the prisoners' shoulders, and tied their wrists to them. They finished their preparations casually. It was another day's work.

True, one of the prisoners was unusual. Jesus of Nazareth

was a Preacher from Galilee. He had been brought to Pilate just that morning by the Jewish leaders. They said He claimed to be king—hardly a believable charge. He had no army and none of the trappings of royalty. Still, the Prisoner and His indictment had provided some great entertainment for the soldiers. Earlier in the day while they had been waiting for Pilate and the priests to finish their haggling, one of them had found a faded purple robe that hinted of past splendor. They draped it around Jesus, braided a crown of thorn branches, jammed it on His head, and shoved a stick into His hands as a scepter. Then they paid mock obeisance.

Ha! A Jewish king? That would be the day! They rose from their knees to spit in His face. Snatching the stick from His hand, they'd hit Him over the head. It had been hilarious.

But you had to admit, this Man was infuriatingly calm. He was hurting; they made sure of that. But He refused to show anger or beg for mercy. He seemed to ignore them. He made fools of them. But they'd show Him. Everyone broke on the cross. He'd be begging for mercy or cursing the pain soon enough.

As the soldiers marched the three convicts away from the prison, their customary pace was slowed by the press of pilgrims in the streets. Then just before they reached the gate on their way out the Preacher collapsed. They hollered at Him and prodded Him, but it was hopeless; He was gone.

Now what? The men looked to Longinus, their commanding officer. "Untie him," he ordered. He whispered to another soldier, who stepped into the edge of the crowd. As this soldier shoved a man to the center, the soldiers breathed a sigh of relief. From his looks and clothes, he had to be a foreigner, someone who'd do what he was told instead of some local hothead who would start a riot.

With a new crossbearer, the soldiers again moved the procession toward Golgotha, accompanied by a heckling mob. The soldiers paid them no mind as long as they did not interfere with the day's work.

On Golgotha, the Place of the Skull, the soldiers continued their well-rehearsed routine. They stripped the accused, fixed them to the boards, and erected the crosses. On the upright above each convict's head, they nailed the placard announcing his crime.

The soldiers took special pleasure in posting the Preacher's placard: JESUS OF NAZARETH, KING OF THE JEWS. It was written in three languages—Latin, Greek, and Hebrew. The soldiers joked to each other under their breath. "Take that, you Jews! See what happens when you challenge Rome!"

One of the perks of doing an execution was the privilege of claiming the convicts' clothes. Not that the clothes of brigands usually amounted to much. Still, in that society any piece of fabric was worth something. As the soldiers divided up the clothes, ripping them to make the portions even, one of them held up Jesus' robe, and protested, "Hey, look you guys, this is too good to rip up. It's woven in one piece. It doesn't have a single seam. What do you say, let's toss for it?"

Somebody pulled dice from his pocket. "Call it." After they put in their bids, he tossed the dice. They all leaned over to see who won. Their congratulations for the winner were mixed with good-natured cursing.

They were finished. The only thing left to do was sit and watch, ensuring that no one rescued the convicts or put them out of their misery prematurely.

The soldiers talked, their minds miles away. Somebody remembered a wrestling match he had watched in Antioch when his troop passed through there. Two soldiers talked about the chariot race coming up in just six weeks on the ides of May at the Coliseum in Rome. One of them went on and on about the new dancing girl he had just seen at Herod's palace; another talked of home and family.

Their part in this drama had been scripted almost a thousand years before. Their use of the nails and their petty gambling for the robe fulfilled exactly the ancient prophecy: "They divide My garments among them, and for My clothing they cast lots" (Psalm 22:18, NKJV).

They were major players in the world's greatest drama, but to the soldiers it was just another day's work. They were watching the Son of God give His life to save the world, and all they saw was a naked convict slowly suffocating. Sitting a few feet from Immanuel, they joked and gossiped, unaware of anything out of the ordinary.

At noon, just as the soldiers were biting into their lunches, Golgotha was engulfed in a bizarre and ominous darkness. It was as if a huge, invisible hand had closed the blinds. An impenetrable blackness pressed down on the crowd. People screamed.

The soldiers stopped eating, food unchewed in their mouths. Something was about to happen. The wailing of the mob filled the blackness as they tried to grope their way back toward Jerusalem, beating their breasts with hands they could not see. As the noise subsided a bit, the soldiers could hear the priests still on Golgotha hissing reproaches and warnings to each other.

"Maybe he'll get away. We should have stoned him the minute we found him."

"I told you guys this was going to lead to no good," another voice said. "Imagine what he'll do for revenge."

The mutterings of the priests about escape and revenge unsettled the soldiers. The penalty for allowing a prisoner to escape was beheading. They edged closer to the crosses, their eyes playing tricks on them as they stared unseeing into the eerie blackness.

Disturbing pictures invaded their reverie. The mocking, the

purple robe, the stick scepter, the crown of thorns—somehow it didn't feel so funny anymore.

While they were nailing Him to the cross, Jesus had neither cursed nor cowered. He did not resist them, yet neither did He appear to be broken. His compliance with their orders was no mere resignation. He acted as though aware of some tremendous presence, as though He and they were all being watched by some august audience. He stretched His arm out for nailing as though consciously following some celestial script rather than merely obeying an executioner's order. In the daylight they had paid no special attention; the man was dirty, bloody, defeated. Now in the blackness with nothing but fear for distraction, the soldiers fought off the sensation that the Preacher was watching them.

Against their will they recalled the Preacher's outburst, "Father, forgive them; they don't understand what they are doing." They'd never heard words like these from a convict before. Who was this Man, anyway?

Was He just another crazy holy man? There were plenty of those around. And this business of "Father, forgive them . . . " What did *they* need forgiveness for anyway? They were just doing their job. Was it any fault of theirs that this fellow could not pull off His scheme to become king? *Who did this man think he was, praying to God for their forgiveness?* That is what they had thought when He said the words. Now with every nerve straining against the unnatural darkness, a retort echoed through their heads, *Who did Pilate think he was sentencing when he sent this man to the cross?*

It was impossible to shake the sense that this darkness was all because of this King. None of the soldiers nor anyone else on Golgotha gave a thought to the thieves in the darkness. Just why or how "the King" and the darkness were connected they didn't know, but the soldiers trembled with an instinctive dread that nature itself was somehow on the side of this Jesus of Nazareth. Maybe His forgiveness was worth something after all.

"Have you heard the stories about the robe?" Longinus asked in a whisper. "Up north in Galilee, Jesus was walking in some big crowd when he suddenly stopped and asked who had touched him.

"The people laughed. 'What do you mean, who touched You? A hundred people must have touched You in the last five minutes.' But this Jesus wouldn't move. 'Somebody touched Me', he insisted. 'I felt power leave Me.' People were getting fidgety, wondering if He had gone mad or something. I mean, there must have been a thousand people in the street.

"Finally, some woman spoke up. 'I touched You, sir.' Seems she'd had some female problem that made her bleed. Had it for twelve years. And you know how these Jewish people are about that kind of thing. She had been an untouchable all that time. Spent all her money on doctors, and nothing helped.

"She told the story right there in front of all those people. She had just touched the Man's robe, she said, and now she knew she was well."

When Longinus finished his story, the men fell silent, brooding. They'd all heard stories about Jesus' healing blind people and epileptics and lepers. They'd even heard that He could raise the dead. This man was different, had been different all day from any other convict they had ever handled. Nature seemed to be on His side. Who was He, really?

For three eternal hours the soldiers stayed at their post, fighting the terror of the unnatural gloom and their fear that something might happen they'd have to answer for.

At last, the darkness began lifting. The terror subsided. Taut muscles began to relax. Again the soldiers were simply standing guard over three dying criminals. But the blackness had permanently altered their commanding officer; it had opened his mind to Jesus of Nazareth. The centurion stared at the King, bewildered, perplexed, entranced. Like everyone else, he had heard stories about this Man. But this afternoon in the darkness, with nature itself testifying to Jesus' uniqueness, Longinus saw something new.

Now in the returning light, Longinus watched Jesus with a fierce intensity. When Jesus called out that He was thirsty, Longinus directed a soldier to give Him a drink using a sponge on a stick. It was crude and pitifully scant help, but it was the best the centurion could do, given his duty.

Not long afterward, Jesus shouted, "It is finished!" then dropped his head. There was a strong earthquake, as though the whole earth was reverberating in answer to Jesus' cry.

The earthquake sealed the growing conviction in Longinus' heart: "Surely," he exclaimed, "this Man was the Son of God." The words were spontaneous; they came straight from the core of his being.

Jesus had won another man to His kingdom. Tradition tells us that this declaration at the cross marked the beginning of a lifelong allegiance to Jesus of Nazareth, the King of the Jews.

There is a sobering message for us in the story of the soldiers. They witnessed the regal dignity of Jesus in His response to the weeping women along the street in Jerusalem. They handled Jesus when He stretched out His arms to the nails— as though embracing his mysterious and grand destiny. Jesus spoke forgiveness for them while they were within earshot. They were present when Jesus comforted His mother and offered paradise to the thief. They were still at Golgotha when nature itself bore testimony to the uniqueness of the Man on the middle cross. But they were oblivious to the cosmic dimensions of the drama in which they were acting a part.

The same kind of thing happens today. People can live with

a Christian spouse, they can take "Bible as literature courses" in college, they can enjoy the splendor and majesty of Yosemite or the Grand Canyon and still be utterly blind to the presence and power of God. But this failure to recognize God's proximity is not limited to people who call themselves agnostics.

We can be baptized, official members of a church, call ourselves by a denominational name, and still receive nothing from Christ. We can even receive Communion and still receive nothing more than did the soldier who won the toss of the dice for Jesus' robe. We can surround ourselves with the mysteries of God in a forest or the grandeur of God in the mountains. White oaks, sugar maples, redwoods, and bald cypress trees all fairly shout the majesty and wisdom of God, but many cannot see the Creator for the trees.

Jesus offers us Himself in baptism, church life, and Communion. He expresses Himself in nature. In a sense, He invites us to touch the hem of His robe by participating in these symbolic expressions of our faith. He invites us to touch and be healed. Jesus offers us Himself in the mystery and wonder of nature. And there, too, the discerning can find the hem of His robe, touch and be healed.

It is easy to come to worship as a spectator. We expect the choir to perform well; we may critique the organist's performance—too much volume, too slow, too loud, too highbrow. We hope the preacher will deliver an engaging, thought-provoking sermon. When we leave, we may analyze the elements of the service—the music, the preaching, the social atmosphere—and be utterly unaware of having been in the presence of God. Like the people thronging Jesus in Galilee or the soldiers sitting at the cross, we are mere spectators.

Sacred symbols can mediate God only to those with open hearts. We need to cultivate attentiveness to God, so that when He reveals Himself through His Word, through baptism, Communion, or nature, we will receive His revelation.

The soldiers passed several hours, first talking and laughing, then cowering, within a few feet of the greatest of all kings, the wisest of all preachers. They heard His words. They watched Him. They heard nothing, saw nothing, of the transcendent. Nature futilely testified to His majesty. The soldiers played dice at the crux of history, oblivious to their opportunity.

We, too, can miss God. Not because He is distant but because we are too preoccupied to notice Him.

But there is good news. Even for someone who has been long in a religious environment, but who has not really encountered Jesus, there is hope. The centurion, one of the men who all afternoon failed to recognize what he was doing and Who he was killing, when he "saw what had happened, glorified God, saying, 'Certainly this was a righteous Man! Truly this Man was the Son of God!'" (Luke 23:47; Mark 15:39).

If you have gone to church, even to Communion, and have not seen God, there is still hope. If you are stubborn in coming into the presence of God where He is lifted up as the crucified Saviour, you may yet join with the centurion in seeing. It took the centurion all day to see, and he was in the immediate, literal presence of Jesus. It may seem to be taking you much too long. But Jesus' graciousness to others, His words, and the testimony of nature will finally breach the barriers in your mind and emotions. Spend the time in His presence, and you will be able to say with glad confidence, "Truly, this Man is the Son of God."

Father,
Forgive Them

" 'Father, forgive them, for they do not know what they are doing' " (Luke 23:34).

The four Gospels record seven statements made by Jesus while He was on the cross. In the centuries following, these statements came to be known among Bible scholars as "The Seven Last Words" of Christ.

None of these statements is in all the Gospels, and none of the Gospels reports all of the statements. Three of them are recorded in Luke, another three in John. One more statement is recorded in both Matthew and Mark.

Why this difference between the respective gospel writers? This diversity of reporting highlights the truth that a sermon is more than just what comes out of the preacher's mouth. A sermon is an interaction between the preacher and the listener. The preacher tells the story of what God has revealed to him; the listeners under the guidance of the Holy Spirit apply it to themselves. The sermon has not been fully delivered until listeners have found the connection between the preacher's story and the story that God is writing in their own lives.

People have come to me after a sermon and thanked me warmly for something helpful they heard in the sermon. And I'm amazed sometimes at what they've heard; it's not something that I intended to say; it's not even something I remember saying.

For these people God took some part of my delivery, which was not central to the sermon as I conceived it, and used it to speak to the listener's heart. The Holy Spirit uses the same sermon to speak to diverse needs. He prompts different people to hear very different truths in the same sermon.

In the same way, each of the Gospel writers recorded those elements in Jesus' teachings and life that struck him most forcefully. Under the direction of the Holy Spirit, each writer reported the statements that helped him make the most sense of the story of Jesus for himself and for his readers.

In this chapter we will examine the first of Jesus' "Seven Last Words."

Before the death march from Pilate's judgment hall to the Place of the Skull, soldiers bloodied Jesus' back with a lash. They rammed a wreath of thorns onto His head, slapped Him around, and hit Him over the head with a stick. They spit in His face and heaped scorn on Him until they ran out of insults. But they had not broken Him. He had maintained absolute silence under the abuse.

On Golgotha they spiked His wrists and ankles to the wood and hoisted Him up against the sky. Pain screamed through His body. He could hold His silence no longer. "Father," He bellowed.

The centurion glanced up. So this strange prisoner had a voice after all. Pain made them all talk—curse, scream, rage. "Father," the Man shouted hoarsely, "Father, forgive them, for they do not know what they are doing."

Did they really not know what they were doing? The soldiers had not spat in His face by accident. The thorns embedded in His scalp did not fall out of a tree. The man with the hammer had driven the nails home through His extremities with grim purpose. To be sure, the crucifixion itself had been decreed by higher authorities. But thorns and spit and blows to the head were gratuitous.

Angels watching the drama were outraged at the abuse. They would have gladly obliterated the tormentors and rescued their King. They were nearly as shocked as the soldiers by His words, "Forgive them."

Do not make the soldiers pay. They are ignorant. They do not know that I alone of all humanity have been holy from the instant of conception. They do not know that I am Immanuel, Saviour, King of kings, Teacher of righteousness, Lamb of God, Jehovah, the I AM, Yahweh, the Prince of Peace, the Everlasting Father, the Good Shepherd. They do not know. How could they? Forgive them.

In their work the soldiers had seen it all. They had wrestled with desperate convicts resisting their crucifixion with almost superhuman strength. They had watched men accept execution with noble resignation. They had crucified whimpering, compliant, broken men. They had heard curses and prayers. But never had they heard a convict pray for them. Never, in all their years, had they encountered love from a man they were torturing.

Foreign soldiers were not the only tormentors that afternoon. They were joined by crowds of Jesus' own people, the people He had left the splendor and joy of heaven to live among. Street toughs and passersby who had joined the taunting, even the chief priests who had engineered this crucifixion—Jesus forgave them all. Jesus forgave His disciples who had let Him down on Thursday night. He forgave Judas for betraying Him. He forgave His friend Peter for his faithless words.

Jesus was not blind to the reality of evil. He loathed it and sternly denounced it. He warned of horrendous consequences for those who stubbornly refused to renounce evil and accept pardon. But as much as Jesus hated evil, He loved human beings even more. He willingly paid with His own life so that people, bad people, could live.

The executioners and the abusive mob had indebted themselves to Jesus. The primeval moral principle—eye for eye and tooth for tooth—decreed that every blow, every jest, deserved retribution. This principle is not merely an attempt by Moses to regulate base human passions. It is a succinct articulation of fundamental, universal law.

Justice and injustice are connected with natural law, but they are more than just impersonal principles. God pledges to personally superintend the distribution of justice. God, as the righteous Judge of all the earth, has obligated Himself to exact vengeance in the name of the victim. Through the apostle Paul we are instructed to "not take revenge, my friends, but leave room for God's wrath, for it is written: 'It is mine to avenge; I will repay'" (Romans 12:19).

It is true that the soldiers at the cross did not know they were killing the Messiah, a perfect human being, the divine Son of God. But the principles of justice were not neutralized by their ignorance. They were committing heinous evil and exposed themselves to appropriate retribution.

But Jesus interrupted the natural chain reaction. He did not allow His blood to call for vengeance. As the victim on the cross, He took the moral debt of His tormentors on Himself: "Father, forgive them. Do not make them pay. I, Myself, choose to absorb the malevolent chain reaction they have launched. They owe Me nothing; I absorb the loss."

When Jesus forgave, He did not pretend that His tormentors had not really hurt Him. He did not excuse their evil. Instead, He, Himself, absorbed the full consequences of their malicious acts. Their evil was deadly; He absorbed the poison and died.

Not everyone valued Jesus' pardon. The priests wanted none of His charity. They had led the chant during Jesus' trial, when Pilate protested they were asking him to condemn an innocent man: "His blood be on us and on our children." One of the thieves cared nothing for the kindness of the dying Preacher. But Jesus released even these ingrates from the eternal consequences of their abuse that afternoon.

"Father, forgive them" created an invitation, a safe house, for everyone on the hill. There is no more heinous crime, no more shameful violation of humanity, than to assault Immanuel, God-in-the-flesh, with intent to kill. And it is precisely this that Jesus forgave.

He endured the pain stabbing at His hands and feet and ballooning in His torso. He took slander and curses and double-crossing. Finally when He could stand it no longer, His whole being erupted, not with curses, not even with complaints, but with "Father, forgive them, for they do not know what they are doing."

These first words of the Preacher from His pulpit created a sanctuary for the hooligans, profane soldiers, corrupt priests, and timid disciples. And some of the priests, soldiers, and hooligans later accepted His pardon. His friends again found joy in His service.

Jesus' words created a sanctuary for us too. We have sinned against the Son of God. Except for His words, we, too, would be exposed to the vengeance of God on His behalf.

Every kindness neglected, every failure to respond graciously and generously to human need—whether it is our wife's, our husband's, our boss's, our neighbor's, our enemy's—is a personal affront to God-in-the-flesh. Every deficiency of love is, in fact, damnable sin.

> " 'Then He will also say to those on the left hand, "Depart from Me, you cursed, into the everlasting fire prepared for the devil and his angels: . . . Assuredly, I say to you, inasmuch as you did not do it to one of the least of these, you did not do it to Me" ' " (Matthew 25:41, 45 NKJV).

We have wounded the Saviour. We have participated in His miserable execution. And we are free because of His pardon.

Have you mistreated Jesus in the person of your children or your brother or sister? Have you destroyed the faith of others by your conduct as a leader in the church? Have you, as a professional, taken advantage of clients? Have you betrayed their confidence? Are you living with remorse and shame so intense that you can tell absolutely no one? Do you go through the motions of church convinced that it is no use, you are damned anyway?

Hear the words of Jesus to those who slapped, nailed, insulted, and scorned Him: "Father, forgive them, for they do not know what they are doing."

Your sin is monstrous. It is worse than you can comprehend. It is so heinous that you cannot really know what you have done. For you Jesus preached the first words of this sermon: "Father, forgive them."

As in any great sermon, in this first statement from the cross, comfort and challenge are blended. We are forgiven, lavishly, affectionately. But we receive this forgivenessonly by allowing it to flow through us. We cannot keep forgiveness for ourselves. We may be conduits of grace, but not reservoirs.

" 'For if you forgive men their trespasses, your heavenly Father will also forgive you. But if you do not forgive men their trespasses, neither will your Father forgive your trespasses' " (Matthew 6:15, NKJV).

People sometimes ask me, "How can I forgive when the slightest reminder of what someone has done fills me with fury? I want to forgive. I've been trying for years to forgive. But how can I forgive when my entire being screams with hurt and outrage?"

One way to move toward forgiveness is to copy the words of Jesus. Instead of trying to say, "I forgive." Pray, "Father, You forgive them."

You may not have the spiritual and emotional strength to forgive, but you can pray to God asking Him to do what you cannot. "Father, You forgive them."

Jesus had the authority to forgive and the spiritual maturity to enable Him to release His tormentors from their responsibility to Him. But instead of announcing forgiveness from Himself, He prayed that His Father would do the forgiving. We can do the same.

Even when we feel that we have neither the authority nor maturity to be able to forgive, we can act as conduits of forgiveness by repeating Jesus' words: "Father, forgive." Using these words, we turn our grievance and the offender over to God by mouthing the right words. Then we trust God to do what is right regarding the offender, and we trust Him to forgive us as we struggle with our feelings.

How big a sin am I expected to forgive? How much hurt can I take before forgiveness becomes unrealistic? Jesus forgave crucifixion and said, " 'I have given you an example, that you should do as I have done to you' " (John 13:15, NKJV).

We may be abused or mistreated at work or by our spouse

or parents or even by our children. And still we can pray Christ's words, "Father, forgive them, for they do not know what they are doing."

Forgiving someone does not mean necessarily that we leave ourselves in the situation. It doesn't mean that we take no action to prevent further damage. It does mean that we turn the injustice over to God, then get on with life, leaving to God the responsibility to attend to justice.

Jesus' first words from the cross set us free from the tyranny of remembered injustice. They set us free from condemnation. They make it clear that it is safe for anyone, for all of us, to come to Jesus, no matter what our past. His intention is to lift our guilt and give us life. If we give Him the slightest chance, He'll do it.

Most Favored Woman:
Mary, Jesus' Mother

Hail, thou that art highly favoured, the Lord is with thee: Blessed art thou among women. Luke 1:27 KJV.

Then Simeon blessed them and said to Mary, his mother: "This child is destined to cause the falling and rising of many in Israel, and to be a sign that will be spoken against, so that the thoughts of many hearts will be revealed. And a sword will pierce your own soul too." Luke 2:34, 35.

Why? Why? Why? The question pounded in Mary's head. Her son was supposed to take David's throne and rule forever. The angel had called her the most blessed of all women. Was this a blessing, to see her Son executed at thirty-three? What of all the prophecies and signs that proved her Son was special?

She sagged against John, her Son's best friend. His arm around her did not take away the pain, but it helped.

This wasn't what she'd expected when the angel first visited her. For a thousand years, every Jewish girl had secretly dreamed of being mother to Messiah. Then Gabriel had visited her and announced that it was going to happen to her! She would, indeed, be the most blessed of all women, the envy of her friends. She had said Yes to the angel. Who wouldn't?

But the excitement quickly faded. As her pregnancy became obvious, the townspeople began to talk. She could have handled that, but when her fiancé talked of breaking off the engagement, she thought she'd die. He was everything to her. At the last minute God saved their relationship by giving Joseph a dream that convinced him she was telling the truth. But it was a narrow escape.

The angel had said, "Greetings, you who are highly favored! The Lord is with you!" But Mary was beginning to wonder if being one of God's favorites was such a good idea after all.

Now here she was, standing in the middle of a violent mob watching her Son die. Where was God in all this? Where was the "favored woman" part of the story?

Back in the village, Joseph had done his best to shield her from the talk of incredulous neighbors, but the looks she got in the market . . . they really hurt. Then had come the trip to Bethlehem. Just as she was due to give birth to the Deliverer of Israel, the One who was going to break the foreign yoke and restore Israel to its rightful supremacy in the world, she and Joseph had been required by the Roman occupation forces to travel from Nazareth to Bethlehem for a tax enrollment. Mary insisted on going. She wasn't going to be left with the sharp tongues in Nazareth.

She remembered the night Jesus was born. The first cradle for the heir to Israel's throne was a feed box! It wasn't right, but they'd survived.

Sometimes God leads us where we would rather not go. There in that stable Mary was not "out of God's will." But she was certainly out of her comfort zone.

Mary remembered the shepherds' visit, how they'd interrupted each other in their excitement while telling their scrambled story. They'd seen a vision of angels, brighter than lightning. Their singing was like waterfalls and wind chimes and thunder and bird song all wrapped together. And they announced that the Saviour of Israel had been born that very evening in Bethlehem! The sign of the new King would be His bed, a manger—a feed box!

Mary could remember her excitement. The secret no longer belonged to just her and Joseph. God was telling others. For sure, the priests would find them soon. Life would get better.

But nothing happened. No one of any consequence paid the slightest attention to the shepherds. Six weeks after Jesus' birth, following the rule for the firstborn, Joseph and Mary took their Son up to the temple in Jerusalem to present Him to God.

Surely, Mary had thought, here in the great center of worship of the true God, the Messiah would be recognized. But when the holy family entered the temple, nothing happened. A priest received their offering of two doves and performed the sacrifice. They watched him write Jesus' name on a large scroll then listened as he droned through a perfunctory blessing.

The priest was just finishing when an old man named Simeon approached, his eyes fixed on the baby. He took Jesus in his arms with such hesitancy and delicacy you'd have thought he was handling butterfly wings. His face glowed as he lifted his eyes and prayed in a quavering voice, "Now, Lord, you can let your servant depart in peace, for my eyes have seen your salvation" (Luke 2:29, 30, paraphrase). Mary never forgot the rapturous wonder in his prayer.

But Simeon did not stop with these heart-thrilling words. He went on to pronounce a cryptic prophecy about Jesus' role as Judge of the nation. Then, turning to Mary, he whispered with a strange mixture of fierceness and solicitude, "And a sword will pierce your own heart also."

What strange words! Every time she heard them, she shivered. Even now, as she stood on Golgotha, the memory chilled her. The angel called her "highly favored"; this old man said, "A sword will pierce your own heart also." Which was true? As she stood there on Golgotha watching her Son die, Simeon's words made sense. Gabriel's didn't.

The "highly favored" had been made more believable some time after Jesus' birth when wealthy strangers from Persia appeared at their door. They had come in quest of the newborn King of the Jews. They had been directed to this house, so they said, by a mysterious star they had first seen in Mesopotamia.

That night Mary had gone to sleep dreaming. Surely now there would be a breakthrough. The strangers had told them King Herod inquired about the Baby. He, himself, wanted to find the Baby and honor Him. At least that's what he said. The gifts the kings brought would make for a comfortable living more in keeping with the true status of their family. She could see in her dream the kind of house they'd have.

Joseph woke her from her dreaming. "Get up, Mary." He was leaning over her, shaking her urgently.

"What time is it?" she mumbled.

"I don't know, the middle of the night sometime. But I just had a dream," he whispered. "An angel told me we must leave town immediately. If we don't, Jesus will be killed. Get up and pack."

She packed and before dawn they were out of town on the road to Egypt.

The strangers' gifts made the trip possible, but they did not provide the kind of comfortable living she had imagined. Then when they heard about the massacre in Bethlehem shortly after they left, she began to comprehend the danger of having a claim to the throne of Israel. Mary and Joseph had to blend in. Even in Egypt they needed to be invisible, part of the crowd. They dared not tell just anyone the stories about angels and shepherds and wealthy strangers from the East. Being favored by God did not mean being appreciated by people.

After some years there, God gave Joseph another dream, directing him to take the family back to Palestine. They finally got back to Palestine, back to their old town of Nazareth, and when Jesus was twelve, they all went up to Jerusalem for the Passover.

With boundless curiosity, Jesus plied every scribe who would listen with questions about the temple service, about Messianic prophecies, about difficult passages in Scripture. Some scribes warmed to His questioning, taking obvious delight in the conversation. Others shook their heads, quickly dismissing the precocious Boy. "You've been doing too much thinking, kid."

They lost Jesus on that trip. Mary and Joseph spent three frantic days looking for Him, wondering if He had been seized by the authorities because someone had connected Him with visit of the Magi.

Throughout the three days, Simeon's words played over and over in her head: "A sword will pierce your own heart also."

They finally found Him: in a back room at the temple, dialoging with learned theologians. When Mary scolded Him for the terror He had caused them, His response again caused her to feel the sword. Not that He was harsh, but He was claiming another Father. He was not theirs alone.

Over the next seventeen years Mary had wondered about the words of the angel, "He will sit on the throne of David. He will reign forever."

What did carving sickle handles and making wagon wheels have to do with ruling the nations with a rod of iron? He needed to get out and make a name for Himself. Nazareth was too small a town for Him.

Still, when He announced it was time to leave, it hurt. She depended on Him. She would miss Him terribly.

She remembered the day Jesus left home. She had worried and swelled with pride all at the same time. Her Son was finally going to demonstrate His royal calling. Before long she'd be known as the mother of a King instead of the widow of a carpenter.

He had gone down to the Jordan where His cousin, John the Baptist, was preaching to crowds of thousands about the Messiah who was going to appear at any time. Thousands of people saw her Son baptized. They heard heaven thunder its approval when He came up out of the river. John had told her that God actually spoke, claiming Jesus as His own Son and declaring His absolute approval.

She began hearing fantastic stories. He drove demons out of people. He gave sight back to blind folk. Epileptics, the lame, people with strange fevers, women with female problems—nothing was too hard for Him. Crowds came to hear Him. She had gone and seen for herself. Once, that she knew of, He fed more than five thousand people with food He produced from a small boy's lunch of bread and fish. Surely this was a prelude to His taking the throne.

But Mary began worrying about her Son's health. People said He was so busy He didn't even take time to eat. He hardly ever slept. What would happen if He had a breakdown? She had enlisted His brothers to come with her and had gone to make Him come home for some home-cooked meals and rest. But once more had come the sword: When she sent a message to Him through the crowd, that she and His brothers would like to see Him, He turned to the crowd and called out, " 'Who is My mother and who are My brothers?" Then waving His hand over the group, He answered His own question. "Here are My mother and My brothers. For whoever does the will of My Father in heaven is My brother and sister and mother' " (Matthew 12:48-50, NKJV).

When Jesus spoke those words, Mary felt the sting of rejection. Just as He had in the temple at age twelve, He defined their relationship. He was in charge. He loved her; He always made that clear. He was honored to be her Son. But He took His orders only from God.

How she delighted to call Him her own. She burst with pride every time she heard another story of His goodness or His power to heal or of the new wisdom someone had found in His teachings. But as time went on, her heart was stabbed when she heard reports of popular dissatisfaction with some of His teachings. Then she began hearing rumors of plots by national leaders to kill Him!

When He left Galilee, this time headed for Jerusalem, Mary decided to go along. If anything happened, she wanted to be close. But she had never imagined this. Crucifixion!

As Mary stood there at the foot of the cross, Simeon's prophecy reached its climax. The sword stabbed to the very core of her being.

A thousand questions must have beat on her mind: What was God doing? What about the shepherds' report and the foreigners' story about the star? What of Simeon's prophecy? The part about her Son being the salvation of Gentiles and Jews? Her Son was hanging on a cross. How did that fit with the angel's promise that God would " 'give him the throne of his father David, and he will reign over the house of Jacob forever; his kingdom will never end' " (Luke 1:32, 33)?

And what about the angel's words, "you who are highly favored"?

Jesus gave her just a bit of an answer even while He was enduring excruciating pain. Looking down at John, Jesus gave her formally into John's charge. He didn't leave her sonless. He didn't leave her to the uncertain kindness of her stepsons. He gave her to the one man who would remind her most of Him.

Yes, she was favored. But she had so many questions. Why did the way of God's favor hurt so much?

When Mary left Golgotha on Friday afternoon, she was utterly crushed and desolate. All God's promises seemed to have failed. She could see no future. Sure, John would take care of her as best he could, but the light of her life was gone. Jesus was dead.

As Mary sat with the friends of Jesus on that Sabbath, her entire world was black and cold. She had no reason to live. No hope. Being favored by God was the last description she'd have thought of using to describe her situation. Cursed felt more like it.

But then came the first reports that Jesus wasn't dead, that He had risen. Along with others, she began recalling statements by Jesus they hadn't understood and hadn't paid much attention to. "I am going to Jerusalem, where I will be handed over to the chief priests. I will be mistreated and killed. But I will rise on the third day." He had tried to tell them. They had just been too thick to understand. The cross wasn't the end.

The angel had not lied. Mary didn't know how, but she was certain that her Son would yet rule. He would triumph. She was no longer concerned about a privileged position in His palace. He had given her the honor of being His mother. He had never allowed her to own Him. She didn't own Him now. But He never let her down; He never abandoned her. She was indeed most favored.

God's favor is often buried in obscure, difficult service. Mary of Nazareth did not enjoy an easier, more comfortable life because she was the mother of Jesus. No one plans to bury their child. It is difficult to imagine a more wrenching experience than watching your only son die on a cross. But looking back from the perspective of eternity, Mary will not regret for an instant that God chose her.

God may give you a very difficult task. You may be called to love a child with attention deficit disorder or autism. Perhaps God has called you to rear three children by yourself or to care for a wife who is permanently disabled.

Maybe your assignment is to remain faithful in a difficult marriage to someone who is not planning to change.

The service God assigns you may not be "fun." In fact, at times it may feel like a curse. You may wonder what you did that so bothered God that He would do this to you. But the obligations of love and service and family are not expressions of God's pique. They are not evidence that you are not favored. Even if it seems there's a sword permanently plunged through your heart, the reality is that God regards you with kindly affection. And painful, difficult service is often proof of His favor.

God has a glorious future for you. And if you are faithful, He one day will greet you with the words, "Whatever you did for the lowliest, you did for me" (Matthew 25:34, paraphrase).

Mary's story in the Bible does not end the Friday of the Crucifixion. It does not end on the Sunday of the Resurrection. Seven weeks later on the day of Pentecost, when the mighty power of God swept over the followers of Jesus, Mary was there. Along with 120 other believers, she received the assurance that through the person of the Holy Spirit, Jesus had joined their company to stay.

After Pentecost Mary finally understood Simeon's prophecy. The sword had pierced her. That part was all too plain. But she understood, too, His prayer, "Lord, now you can let your servant depart in peace, for I have seen your salvation." Pricked so many times throughout Jesus' life her soul, at Golgotha, had been brutally stabbed. But now she saw clearly the salvation of God.

Jesus, the God-man, had given her the privilege of being His mother. She had borne Him, nursed Him, taught Him to read. She had watched her Son die. She, more vividly than anyone else in the whole world, remembered Him. He had been hers. Now, she was His. And He was alive forever. She was indeed favored, blessed above all women.

WOMAN,
THERE IS YOUR SON

Near the cross of Jesus stood his mother, his mother's sister, Mary the wife of Clopas, and Mary of Magdala. When Jesus saw his mother there, and the disciple whom he loved standing nearby, he said to his mother, "Dear woman, here is your son," and to the disciple, "Here is your mother." From that time on, this disciple took her into his home (John 19:25-27).

Jesus declared, "Who is my mother, and who are my brothers?" Gesturing toward the crowd of his adherents, he continued, "Here are my mother and brothers" (Matthew 12:48, 49, paraphrase).

Jesus was already weak when they marched Him out of Jerusalem. Now, the trauma of the cross—both physical and spiritual—was quickly draining any life He had left. His eyes closed; He was fighting for every breath. John stood with Jesus' mother, Mary, right at the foot of the cross. They were surrounded by the hostile crowd.

Jesus opened His eyes and saw them. He tried to moisten

His lips with His dry tongue then spoke to Mary. "Ma'am," He gestured with His eyes toward John, "there is your son." He panted, trying to catch His breath. Looking at John and nodding His head toward Mary, He said quietly, "There is your mother."

These words of Jesus from the cross do not sound like theology. They seem to contrast sharply with the profound discourses on true worship, judgment, the authority and dignity of the Son of man, eternal life, and the Holy Spirit, which comprise a large part of John's Gospel. The fact is, however, these words of Jesus to Mary and John express the very core of Christian theology.

In the first chapter of his book, John gives one of the most vivid descriptions in the Bible of Jesus' divinity: Before He appeared on earth as Jesus, the "Word" shared eternal existence and divine prerogatives with God the Father. Every act of divine creation involved Him. Then comes the startling truth. This Being, the Word, became human and lived among us, exhibiting in human form the graciousness and wisdom of God.

Christian theology is not ideas about "a God up in the sky" or a system of rituals or beliefs that will somehow enable us to attain perfection and enter bliss. Rather, it is the story of *the* "God up in the sky" who came and lived among us, as one of us. The religion of Jesus is love in action. It is concrete. It is tangible spirituality.

Jesus' love for humanity was not merely nice feelings. He did not just wish us well from a distant, comfortable throne. Nor did He come to earth merely as a tourist or as a preacher. He became part of our world; He was a significant participant.

While here on earth Jesus did not just talk, though every word He said mattered and was true. He acted. He did things that spoke as loudly as His words—things that confirmed and illuminated His words. When one of His disciples had a question about who He really was, Jesus replied, in essence, "I am just who I have been telling you—a perfect complement of My Father in heaven. But if you find My words hard to accept or understand, just look at what I've been doing. Consider the blind people who see, the congenitally lame who now walk, the dead who are living again, the sinners who have been given new life. If My words aren't persuasive, My actions will convince you for sure" (John 14:11, paraphrase).

In three and a half years of preaching and healing, Jesus changed humanity's understanding of God. He created a vivid, new picture of God. But it was not enough. Humanity was still enslaved. Despite our new insight into the character of God, we were still mortgaged to our past, to the devil, and to our own brokenness. The law of retribution still decreed our doom. So Jesus took the ultimate step to rescue us. He died to set us free.

By His death He paid off the mortgage; He redirected the retribution. He created a new future for us; He opened opportunities that apart from His death simply did not exist for human beings. Jesus' love for humanity was neither vapid sentimentality nor cold, aloof "doing this for your own good." Rather, His love combined warm, affectionate regard for each human with the toughness needed to act genuinely in our best interest, in the face of evil.

This blend of affection and toughness was illustrated in Jesus' interaction with Mary and John. Jesus was suffering on the cross in order to benefit the entire human race. He would not be turned from His global objective by the grief His work caused His mother and friends. Sympathy for hurting people did not make Him irresolute in fighting and winning the cosmic war.

On the other hand, He paused in His battle with sin and

the devil to personally arrange care for His mother. He did not allow His global obligations to distract Him from His personal, familial duties.

Jesus' words to John and Mary are theology, that is, they are words about God. They indicate God's profound interest in, and concern for, each individual.

Jesus called His disciples to follow His lead.

> My commandment is this: love one another, just as I love you. . . . You are my friends if you do what I command you. . . . This, then, is what I command you: love one another. John 15:12, 14, 17, TEV.

At the heart of Christianity is the command to love people according to the model created by Jesus of Nazareth. It is not enough to feel compassion for the victims we see on the evening news; we must act compassionately. It is not enough to give money to church programs that help the needy or preach the gospel. We must ourselves, personally, do for people in the name of Christ. It's insufficient to believe that "God so loved the world. . . ." We are to pass on in tangible ways the love we have received. Jesus commanded us to love; it is not optional. And He demonstrated what He meant by love when He spoke from the cross to His mother.

In our society, with our high mobility, it is common for work to take us away from our extended families. Pastors and parochial school teachers are especially mobile, moving every few years. But professional religious workers must not allow distance or the demands of "God's work" to divert them from their obligations to their parents.

Jesus' words from the cross set the standard for caring for our parents when ministry takes us from them. Jesus did not leave Mary to fend for herself. He did not leave Her to the uncertain care of her stepsons, the people who "should" have taken care of her. Jesus made certain that she would be cared for by someone who loved her.

If we accept Jesus' life as the definitive illustration of a spiritual life, that is, a life lived consciously vis-à-vis God, we are confronted with the truth that spiritual life cannot be limited to "spiritual" activities like prayer, meditation, Bible study, worship, and preaching the gospel. Spiritual life will, without exception, include down-to-earth service to our mothers and fathers and siblings and children.

In Jesus' day, religious conservatives had a tradition that could be used to provide a religious cover for neglecting one's parents. It was called "corban." According to this tradition, if a person dedicated his assets to God, he could retain personal use of them as long as he lived. But his assets were unavailable to any other persons. So a man could explain to his parents, "I'd love to help you, but I don't have any money. All my assets have been dedicated to God."

Jesus challenged this practice. " 'Why do you break the commandment of God for the sake of your tradition?' " He asked. " 'God said, "Honor your father and mother." You say, "Neglect them." So you nullify the word of God for the sake of your tradition' " (Matthew 15:3-7, paraphrase).

Theology, worship, and even philanthropy are pointless if unaccompanied by fidelity in our relationship with our parents.

The early Christian church picked up this teaching of Jesus and made it a pillar of their corporate life. The apostle Paul wrote, "If anyone does not provide for his relatives, and especially for his immediate family, he has denied the faith and is worse than an unbeliever" (1 Timothy 5:8).

The church altered the definition of family. It continued to respect the fundamental family unit, but it also understood itself to be a family, taking its cue from the words of Jesus:

"Who is my mother, and who are my brothers?"
Pointing to his disciples, he said, "Here are my mother
and my brothers. For whoever does the will of my
Father in heaven is my brother and sister and mother"
(Matthew 12:48-50).

In the early days of Christianity in Jerusalem, this sense of the
church as family was so strong that they practiced something close
to community of property (Acts 2:44; 4:32-37; 5:4). This
semicommunalism was not practiced across the empire as Christianity spread, nor did it endure in Jerusalem. But for the first two
hundred fifty years of church history, the mutual care of Christians for each other was one of the distinguishing marks of the
church Jesus founded. The church took seriously Jesus' teaching:
" 'Whatever you did for one of the least of these brothers of mine,
you did for me.' " (Matthew 25:40).

One of the pithiest statements of the inseparability of Christian theology and tangible compassion is in the book of James:

What God the Father considers to be pure and genuine religion is this: to take care of orphans and widows
in their suffering and to keep oneself from being cor-
rupted by the world (James 1:27, TEV).

James wrote his brief book for people who preferred to con-
ceive of Christianity as a philosophy, as ideas about God and
sin and salvation. The gospel is certainly words about God. It
is the good news that God is for us, that He has redeemed us
from sin and death and the devil. But it is also "the power of
God." And our response to the gospel must be more than nodding our heads and saying, "Yes, that is true." Disciples of
Jesus will incarnate His love.

The call for concrete religion, a religion of action, is presented just as forcefully by John and Paul (famous as theologians) as it is by Matthew and James (famous for their instructions on how to live).

If the New Testament is authoritative, there is no escaping the fact that Christianity cannot be only a matter of thinking, believing, and feeling; Christianity means taking action—first of all for those nearest us. Christian spirituality cannot be confined to religious activities. It inevitably expresses itself in mundane service.

This view of life directly contradicts a major trend in American society—the notion that regard for one's own well-being is the preeminent value. This trend is expressed to varying degrees in things like divorce, abandonment of parents, child abuse, and cocooning.

People in our society work hard. Many professionals routinely work sixty to eighty hours a week. Many people work even more—keeping up with their career or holding down two or three jobs just to pay the rent and buy groceries and shoes for the kids. In the face of this pressure, when we can finally go home, we want to escape. We want to tune out the world and relax. As we seek relief from the stresses of the work world, we are tempted to ignore any relationship that does not contribute to our comfort.

"Leave me alone!" would serve nicely as the motto for these overworked people. But Jesus challenges us: "Is your work more important than saving the world? On an afternoon when I was literally saving the world, I took the time and energy necessary to arrange care for My mother. Can you not take the time from your career or practice or company or church or job to personally care for your parents or neighbors or friends?"

On the radio recently, a well-known writer and speaker declared in an interview: "We were not put here to take care of our parents." While it is true that care for our parents is not the all-encompassing definition of life's purpose, such care is an inescapable part of our purpose in life. We were, indeed, put here to help care for our parents. When a wealthy young man came to Jesus wanting to know what life was all about, Jesus included in His response a quotation from the Ten Commandments: " 'Honor your father and mother' " (Luke 18:20).

The call to love means a call to involve ourselves with people who need us. That begins with our own family, then includes our church family and our neighborhood, our nation, and the world.

Christians who have become feeble and perhaps senile are no less our brothers and sisters, mothers and fathers. Kindness shown to them is kindness shown to the siblings and parents of Jesus Christ. In the eyes of the world it may be wasted energy, futile service; in the eyes of heaven it is appropriate love.

When we accept Jesus' call to love sacrificially, we discover hidden treasures. When Jesus asked John to take charge of His mother for Him, He not only gave John an obligation, He gave him a high privilege. Having Mary in his home was like having a piece of Jesus back again. John counted Jesus his best friend. He felt a huge debt of gratitude to Jesus. So every time he extended himself in caring for Mary, he had the pleasure of making another small payment on that unpayable debt. He had no ambition to eliminate the debt, but it was a rich privilege to "make payments" to his friend.

"Woman, there is your son. John, there is your mother." In these simple words Jesus demonstrated His care for individuals. He genuinely cares about us. And He calls us to represent Him in caring for others.

He Sinned His Way to God:
The Repentant Thief

Then one of the criminals who were hanged blasphemed Him, saying, "If You are the Christ, save Yourself and us." But the other, answering, rebuked him, saying, "Do you not even fear God, seeing you are under the same condemnation?" . . . Then he said to Jesus, "Lord, remember me when You come into Your kingdom" (Luke 23:39-40, 42, NKJV).

What wasted lives! We know nothing certain about the two men except their occupation: thieves. Even their names had to be invented by ancient storytellers. The legends from the second century A. D. named one of them Dysmas. In sacred history, the whole of Dysmas's life was reported in a single sentence. He was a thief, not a glamorous Robin Hood or famous bandit, just an ordinary thief, a ne'er-do-well.

As Dysmas and his friend were marched out of the jail to the place of execution, a weird preacher type was added to the procession. Dysmas had heard of Him; who hadn't? But he never dreamed he would meet Him. The thief was startled by the Preacher's appearance. The Man looked like death warmed over, blood on His face and neck from the thorns in His scalp, blood soaking through His clothes from lacerations on His back. They must have really worked Him over.

The noise was frightful. Crucifixions always drew a crowd of onlookers, and often they were hostile. Jerusalemites hated the Romans for introducing crucifixion to their country, but they hated crooks even more. Today, though, something was different. It seemed to Dysmas that there was a kind of orchestration in the mob's noise and crudeness. They were really working over the Preacher man. Could this whole thing have been staged?

On Golgotha, Dysmas, along with his partner and Jesus, was spiked to his cross and hoisted into space. Pain exploded through his arms and feet. After some time, the pain no longer commanded all his attention. He began hearing the crowd's relentless taunts.

At least, he thought, *they're not after me.*

"Hey, Jesus," someone in the crowd yelled, "if you come down, I promise I'll believe you. Cross my heart, hope to die."

A short, skinny man with a high-pitched voice sniffed, "He saved others, isn't it amazing that he cannot save Himself."

"He said he could build the temple in three days," someone else piped up. "Hey, preacher, won't it be kind of hard to build something with your hands nailed down?" Snickers and loud, crude laughs followed each new insult.

"Hail, mighty king," called a heckler, interrupting himself with his own snorting laughter, "Hail, king. You walked on water. In fact, I heard that you supposedly stopped a whole storm all by yourself. Where's all your power now?"

Dysmas and his buddy joined the jeering. It felt better to throw insults than to face their own smothering despair. Dysmas tried not to think of all the choices he could have made that would have spared him this end. The curse of God—

that's what people called it. Anyone hung on a tree was cursed. A cross was the ultimate cursed tree. And why shouldn't he be cursed?

He remembered the time he and his friend had knocked down an old lady on her way to market. She didn't have any money, just a sack of apricots. They had each stuffed a few into their bags and left her cowering in the dirt. What for? Why did he have to beat up grandmas?

Pictures of his first murder played in his mind. A group of his friends had jumped a fellow. He looked as if he was thirteen or fourteen. They figured he had money. He made too much trouble, and one of the group put a dagger in the fellow's back just below his ribs. They got his money, all right—quite a bit, in fact. But was it worth spilling the guy's guts? Dysmas had gotten used to doing what was necessary, but he could never quite put to sleep the memory of that first time.

Dysmas shook his head, trying to escape the sickening memories.

"Hey, preacher man," he grunted, "why don't you get yourself out of this mess and take us with you? I know a great hideout just a half day's run from here."

Later as the pain began to rise in his viscera and shoulders, his jibes at the Preacher became fiercer. "Hey, preach, did ya really do all that stuff they been saying? Then why don't you do something, huh? Get us out of here!" His actual words were too profane to write.

"Quit hanging there like a side of beef and do something!"

Both thieves were becoming crazed with pain. The Preacher between them made a perfect target for their fury at God and the world and their pain. His silence annoyed and provoked them. Goaded by pain, the crowd, and each other, their language grew even harsher and more vulgar.

Finally the man in the middle broke His silence. Looking

down at a sobbing woman, He called to her, "Lady." She raised her head. Lifting His right eyebrow and glancing with His eyes at the man standing beside her, He rasped, "Lady, there's your son." He paused, caught his breath then spoke again, this time tilting His head toward the woman, "There is your mother."

Dysmas was stunned. He hadn't paid much attention to the quiet people about the cross. There were too many noisy ones. Well, he had noticed one striking lady he took to be the Preacher's mistress or wife. Now he looked around and saw huddled groups of people out on the edges of the crowd obviously distraught because the man next to him was dying.

It was not unusual for a convict to have friends or relatives. But the Preacher's interaction with that man and woman at the foot of His cross gripped Dysmas's attention. Even though His words were distorted by pain and the dryness of His mouth, there was a gentleness and warmth in the Preacher's voice utterly alien to this miserable place. It was from another universe.

The thief had heard the Preacher speak when the three were first nailed to their crosses. But Dysmas had been too busy with his own pain to pay much attention. Now the words came back to him: "Father, forgive them, for they do not know what they are doing."

What kind of man was this who remained free even on a cross? After all they had done to Him, He still was not broken. He acted like a king dispensing royal favors, not a defeated convict. He acted like a god distributing mercy. This Preacher who could not be cowed began to stir respect in the thief.

Dysmas listened with fresh interest to the priests in the crowd. He had never trusted anyone, especially religious people. If they were against this Preacher, maybe He was really OK. For Dysmas, the renegade, it was not too hard to sympathize with someone the system hated.

Besides, was the stuff they were saying really true? Had this Man really, truly raised the dead, walked on water, and created huge picnics from little boys' lunches? If He had, why were the priests so down on Him? Ordinary men did not do those things. Could the rumors that He was the Messiah be true?

The thief began to resent the taunts against the Preacher. The laughs of these religious people didn't sound that different from the laughs Dysmas used to hear when his gang beat up someone. Something about their fury was unnatural.

Without realizing it, Dysmas had changed sides. His buddy on the third cross, however, was still going full steam, blasting the royal Preacher whenever he could spare enough energy from fighting for breath. Dysmas turned on him.

"Shut up, you fool," he rasped, "Leave him alone. We deserve what we are getting, but this guy hasn't done anything wrong. He's innocent."

The longer Dysmas watched, the more convinced he was that the silence of the man beside him was a mask for strength. Dysmas could have resisted brute force, but this man's strength, coupled with the gentleness He showed toward His mother—that was something else.

Something strange was happening to Dysmas. He knew nothing about this new sensation welling up in him. For perhaps the first time in his entire life, Dysmas trusted someone. For the first time in his life, he found himself wanting to give first place to someone else, to a man worthy of his loyalty. He could hardly believe the words that came out of his own mouth: "Remember me when You come in Your kingdom."

Jesus' reply was broken by His own gasps for breath. But the words were unmistakable: "I tell you today, you will be with me in paradise."

Jesus struggled to get the words out. He was farther gone than His neighbors. "Rest easy, friend. I have a place reserved for you. Since you've offered Me yourself, I guarantee it right now, there's a place for you." Jesus smiled when he said "friend" and nodded His head ever so slightly before wrenching with another spasm of pain.

There on that hill, in a place of execution, Jesus made a friend among thieves.

What is the message for us in this story? Just this: Jesus can take the totality of your life and recycle it into a treasure.

In recycling, one of the most crucial steps is separation. Not everything can be recycled. Some things, like paint containers, are irredeemable trash, fit only for a landfill or incinerator. They must be separated out. Without separation at some point, earthly recycling does not work.

In God's recycling operation, however, separation is not the key. There are no people nor any part of a person's life that God cannot recycle. Starting with our lives as they are, including the most bizarre and useless elements of our personalities and histories, God can create a tapestry of remarkable beauty and utility. The only things God does not recycle are what we refuse to put in the bin.

On Golgotha that afternoon, Jesus as the great recycler, transformed a brigand into a friend of God and a model of grace.

But Jesus did more than just make a friend. The Son of God did more than save a man from hell, more than make a saint out of a reprobate. He gave back to a thief the entirety of his life as something he could keep for all eternity.

When the thief first yielded to Jesus, he must have been swamped with remorse. His entire life seemed a waste—mistakes, bad choices, futile rebellions, harmful acts. He would have been delighted for God to simply erase his whole life from the heavenly videotapes.

But his desire for oblivion was contradicted by his friendship with Jesus. Which episode in his life could be omitted and he still end up meeting Jesus and becoming his friend? That friendship now comprised the supreme value in his life. The worth of everything was measured by its impact on that friendship. His most recent arrest, which had led directly to crucifixion, had brought him here to Golgotha to meet Jesus. The thief's gravest mistake, the wrongdoing that led directly and inescapably to his death, also brought him face to face with Jesus. Not for anything would he undo that!

Did God intend for Dysmas to steal and die? No, absolutely not, but over and over, the Bible writers tell of God's taking not just people's best efforts, but their greatest blunders and even their gravest sins and weaving those disasters back into His plan. And He does it in such a masterful way that, looking back from the viewpoint of eternity, it will appear that God planned and orchestrated it all. Even while sinners are hard at work rebelling against Him, God is working in their foolishness to accomplish His beneficent purposes.

God's goodness shames us. We hate the damage our wrongdoing has done to people and the disgrace it has brought on God. But when we see what God has made of our lives, we cannot hate ourselves without somehow denigrating Him.

Have you made a mess of your life? Have you ruined God's plan for your life? Gotten into an unwise marriage? Contracted AIDS? Alienated your children? Allowed an illicit sexual union to invade your life? Have you neglected your spiritual life or broken your connection with the church of God?

Have you gone so far away from God's ideal for your life that nothing can be done? Don't you believe it. God's plan for your life always begins exactly where you are right now. God is eager to receive you. If you will give Him your life in its entirety—mistakes, sins, and good times alike—He will re-weave it so that from the perspective of eternity it will appear to have been wholly under His sovereign direction.

Even if you are nailed to a cross that you have fully earned, God is not made helpless. Even if you have deliberately caused the difficulties that now stand between you and God, God will make a way for you to walk again in His company, a way that begins in your present situation.

God is eager for us to pray the thief's prayer: "Lord, remember me when you come into your kingdom." If we will cry for that kind of help, we are assured of God's response: "I tell you today, you will be with me in paradise."

PARADISE GUARANTEED

The thief said to Jesus, "Lord, remember me when you come into your kingdom." Jesus answered, "You can count on it; I promise you today, you will be with me in Paradise" (Luke 23:42, 43, paraphrase).

One of the distinguishing characteristics of Luke as a writer is the special attention he gives in his book to "nobodies," to people with no status. He gives much more detail about Jesus' birth than the other three Gospel writers; he writes more about Jesus' ministry to women and children. He recounts the most compelling stories about Jesus' ministry to society's outcasts. Luke's inclusion of Jesus' words to the repentant thief fits this pattern.

The first words of Jesus on the cross recorded by Luke were " 'Father, forgive them, for they do not know what they are doing' " (Luke 23:34).

When Jesus spoke these words in the presence of Roman soldiers—people utterly beyond the mercy of God, according to current popular opinion—He was expressing again the same truth He had declared earlier in His ministry: " 'The Son of

Man did not come to destroy men's lives but to save them' "
(Luke 9:56, NKJV); "The Son of Man has come to seek and
to save that which was lost" (Luke 19:10, NKJV).

Jesus was in the business of saving, restoring, reclaiming.
Sinners were His special interest, people who were genuinely,
thoroughly evil. His preaching, His healing ministry, His dying—all were intended to save human beings permeated with
evil. Jesus was interested in the entire human race; His compassion was universal. He preached to thousands, and His death
was the punishment that expiated "the iniquity of us all" (Isaiah
53:6). But He also gave attention to specific individuals—a
chief tax collector in Jericho, a reformed prostitute in Bethany,
a devout Jewish ruler in Jerusalem, and a thief on an adjacent
cross on Golgotha.

Jesus' first words from the cross, "Father, forgive them,"
expresses heaven's attitude toward sinners en masse. The second statement Luke records shows us God's keen interest in a
particular person.

God has planted eternity in our hearts. It is in our very
nature to long for the future. Some people, Christians included,
who have lived very long and whose health is failing, finally
reach the point where they are ready to let go of life, but they
do so looking to the future, longing for their friends who have
died. God did not put this longing for the future in us to tease
us. He intended for it to impel us to seek Him, and we will
find Him if we really look (Jeremiah 29:13).

And God does not expect us to spend our lives guessing
whether or not we have found Him, wondering if we have a
secure future. We can have confidence of eternal life now. The
New Testament is full of reassuring words:

> If you confess with your mouth the Lord Jesus and
> believe in your heart that God has raised Him from

the dead, you will be saved. . . . For "whoever calls upon the name of the LORD shall be saved" (Romans 10:9, 13, NKJV).

"All that the Father gives Me will come to Me, and the one who comes to Me I will by no means cast out. For I have come down from heaven, not to do My own will, but the will of Him who sent Me. . . . And this is the will of Him who sent Me, that everyone who sees the Son and believes in Him may have everlasting life; and I will raise him up at the last day" (John 6:37-40, NKJV).

Also I say to you, whoever confesses Me before men, him the Son of Man also will confess before the angels of God. . . . Do not fear, little flock, for it is your Father's good pleasure to give you the kingdom (Luke 12:8, 32, NKJV).

Humble yourselves before the Lord, and he will lift you up (James 4:10).

God delights in giving us certainty about our future. To be sure, the message of the judgment, which is reiterated throughout the New Testament, should check any frivolity in our response to God. God is not a "nice guy" so timid and eager to please that He can be intimidated or badgered into giving eternal life to people who reject His sovereignty. But the gospel shouts from nearly every page: God is pleased to give us the kingdom. If we call on Him, He will save us. We can count on it. If today I call on God for salvation, I can be certain that God has heard me and that my future is secure. The Bible does not lie: Whoever believes in the Son has eternal life (John 3:36).

Our security is not in the purity or wholeheartedness of our confession. It is not the strength of our faith that saves us. It is God who saves. It is God who will finish the inner work that must be accomplished in our lives. It is the power of God that keeps our salvation secure. And God is no shirker.

> Blessed be the God and Father of our Lord Jesus Christ, who according to His abundant mercy has begotten us again to a living hope through the resurrection of Jesus Christ from the dead, to an inheritance incorruptible and undefiled and that does not fade away, reserved in heaven for you, who are kept by the power of God through faith for salvation ready to be revealed in the last time (1 Peter 1:3-5, NKJV).

> I am sure that God, who began this good work in you, will carry it on until it is finished on the Day of Christ Jesus (Philippians 1:6, TEV).

When the thief cried out, "Lord, remember me when you come into your kingdom," Jesus gave a strong, unequivocal answer NOT merely because the thief was about to die. Jesus gave him an emphatic, positive assurance of a place with Him in paradise because He knew the thief was not playacting, and because He Himself was prepared to make sure that the thief was, in fact, saved.

Jesus offered this guarantee before the thief had an opportunity to prove the sincerity of his desire to reform his life, before he could repay the people he had robbed. If the thief had lived, he would have made restitution to the best of his ability; he would have renounced his thieving ways. He would have lived a godly life. But his acceptance into the kingdom of God was not based on a reformed life. He was made a citizen of heaven because he called on Jesus for salvation. Jesus could offer him citizenship because He was Himself that day taking the thief's deserved punishment.

Jesus' offer of eternal life to us is no less definite, no less immediate than it was to the thief. If today we call on the Lord Jesus, we can be sure, today, of eternal life.

Traditional understanding of Jesus' words to the thief sees Him as guaranteeing the thief an immediate entrance into paradise that day. That would be comforting for the thief, but it would be of little value to modern Christians seeking certainty in their own desire for paradise. Unless we were facing certain, imminent death, Jesus' words would not apply to us. But understood properly, these words speak directly to everyone who is considering calling on Jesus. To all of us Jesus is prepared to respond immediately, today, with a promise of eternal life.

The "today" in Jesus' words refers to Jesus' promise, not the thief's entrance into paradise. Jesus was, that very moment, promising the thief paradise. "Today, right now, while you're still hanging on a cross, scorned by your society and apparently rejected by God, this very minute, I give you my word that you are accepted as a citizen of the kingdom. Because you have put your confidence in Me, I will not allow anyone to snatch you from My hand."

For some people, the supposedly universal desire for eternity is eclipsed by their hunger for acceptance. They struggle with a profound sense of unworthiness or incompleteness or alienation. They don't want more time in their lives. They want more friends, more love, a greater sense of connection to someone who truly cares about them. They ask, "Why should I want to live forever? An eternity of feeling as I do now would be hell."

Jesus' words to the thief speak directly to this hunger for acceptance. "I promise you today, you will be *with me* in paradise."

At that moment the thief was at the low point of attractiveness or worthiness. The process of crucifixion made people ugly. The men were stripped naked. They bled and sweated and performed their bodily functions. The steadily increasing pain distorted their features. Crucifixion itself represented profound rejection by society, even execration (in the archaic sense of invoking a curse upon). The thief had earned this execution; he was not framed.

It was with a crucified man, a bloodied, dirty, exposed and cursed thief, whom Jesus promised to share His kingdom. Jesus did not offer the thief merely a place in heaven. He did not say, "You can go there. Have a good time. See you later." Jesus offered the thief fellowship *with Himself.* "You will be *with me* in paradise."

Jesus is interested in you too. He desires your company in paradise. He told His disciples, "Fear not, little flock; for it is your Father's good pleasure to give you the kingdom" (Luke 12:32, KJV). He meant His words for you too. God the Father and God the Son request the honor of your presence at the inaugural feast of the kingdom of God. Amazingly, they really mean it. They will be honored by your presence!

You may respond, "They couldn't possibly desire the honor of *my* presence. You don't know *me.* You don't know all the stuff I've done. You can't imagine the extent of my failures, my weaknesses, my wickedness."

True, I don't know about you, but God does, and He still insists it is His good pleasure to have you with Him in His kingdom.

Many pastors struggle with a profound sense of inadequacy. They preach the gospel, they visit, they care about people, they serve people. But they are haunted by the goals they have not achieved, people they have not won over, mistakes they have made.

These hard-working servants of God need to hear the words of Jesus to the thief, "You will be with me in paradise." Jesus accepts them before they have met their goals, before they have mastered every skill, before they have impressed every parishioner.

In the society of Jesus and the thief, the cross was the ultimate statement of scorn and denigration. Many believed that crucifixion was proof a person was cursed by God. The thief's own conscience condemned him. The only thing that gave him hope were the words of Jesus, "Today I tell you, you will be with me in paradise."

There are people today in an analogous position. Perhaps you're dying of AIDS, which you contracted through promiscuity. Your conscience condemns you. The church condemns what you've done. Your body, wasted by the disease, has lost all attractiveness. But if you call on the name of the Lord, you will be saved. You will receive the same assurance as the thief, "I promise you today, you will be with me in paradise."

Jesus' words to the thief emphasize the truth that society's verdict against you, the condemnation of your conscience, rejection by your parents or employer or friends—none of these can alienate God from you. Jesus accepted the thief. He wants to accept you. These words of Jesus on the cross apply to you no matter who you are. Whoever calls on the name of the Lord will be saved—not grudgingly, not reluctantly, but with great pleasure.

Drug addicts and sex offenders, adulterers and liars, pastors and church leaders, teenagers and octogenarians—all are eagerly welcomed by God the Father, God the Son, God the Holy Spirit, and the company of heaven's angels. Jesus wants us to know this when we recall His response to the thief: "I promise you today, you will be with me in paradise."

Heaven has a place for you. And for your friends. And for your enemies. It is the Father's good pleasure to give you the kingdom. Don't turn Him down.

A Great Pharisee:
Nicodemus

There was a man of the Pharisees named Nicodemus, a ruler of the Jews. . . . Jesus . . . said to him, "Most assuredly, I say to you, unless one is born again, he cannot see the kingdom of God."

And Nicodemus, who at first came to Jesus by night, also came, bringing a mixture of myrrh and aloes, about a hundred pounds (John 3:1, 3; 19:39, NKJV).

Two men stood on the edge of the crowd at Golgotha, both obviously upper class but, just as obviously, not connected with the hostile dignitaries clustered near the cross.

The older man was Nicodemus, known throughout the country for his scholarship and righteousness. The other was Joseph. His family came from a small village called Arimathea. Both were members of the Sanhedrin, the Jewish ruling council.

Nicodemus hounded himself with remorse. Why had he waited? What had he gained by hiding his appreciation of Jesus of Nazareth? He had allowed Caiaphas and his allies to steal, through intimidation, the richest opportunity of his life. Nicodemus had been scared away from conversation and collaboration with Jesus.

For three years Nicodemus had been a secret admirer, with emphasis on *secret*. He had put off signing on the dotted line with the most incredibly good Person he had ever met. Now his chance was gone. Jesus was dying.

It had seemed so reasonable. By staying in the political mainstream, Nicodemus thought he could blunt attacks on Jesus. Jesus needed a friend in high places, and Nicodemus aimed to be that friend. Sure, it had meant masking his appreciation; it meant limiting his contact with Jesus. But, he'd reasoned, that was a small price to pay for the opportunity to advance the cause of righteousness in the nation. By remaining aloof from Jesus, he kept his seat on the council; he maintained his social contacts, his status. But it had all been a waste. All his subtlety, all his strategy and calculation, were down the drain. Jesus was dying, and there was nothing he could do now to stop it.

The emergency meeting of the council this morning would have been one time when Nicodemus could have used the power and respect he had acquired through forty years of public life. He could have really made a difference. He would have gladly called in every I-owe-you to influence the decision. But the enemies of Jesus outwitted him by calling an illegal, extraordinary session of the Sanhedrin without notifying him. He, and Joseph, too, slept through the most important meeting in the history of the Sanhedrin. Now it was too late.

So Joseph and Nicodemus stood at the edge of the crowd on Golgotha and bore silent witness against the injustice.

Joseph interrupted his thoughts. "You met Jesus once, didn't you?"

"Yes, just once, early on. I only wish I'd met Him more

often. You know, sometimes you do what seems like the prudent thing only to find you've been a fool. I was afraid of losing my influence in the council. I thought God needed me there." Nicodemus paused, then added ironically, "A lot of good I did."

"But God did use you," Joseph protested. "You know He did. Last year during the Feast of Tabernacles when Caiaphas tried to arrest Jesus and the officers came back empty-handed, saying they'd never heard anyone like Him. Caiaphas exploded, remember? He tried to railroad through a motion condemning Jesus right then. It would have carried, too, if you hadn't spoken up. They'd have killed Him that week. Don't be so hard on yourself. You saved Him at least once. That's more than I can say for myself."

"True, Joseph," Nicodemus responded wearily, "I do believe God used my protest in that meeting. But where was I this morning when they voted? Sound asleep in bed. If God needed me in the Sanhedrin, then why didn't He wake me up and get me to the meeting? God used me last year. True. God can use any fool. I've been a fool, Joseph. We've both been fools.

"Look, Joseph, what have we accomplished? The Man is dying. And think what we've missed. We could have gone to hear Him preach. We could have watched Him touch lepers. We could have taken friends to see Him, to hear Him. We could have learned from Him. Instead, we sat around arguing with priests who've bought their offices and rabbis whose primary concern is their perks. We imagined we were protecting Him by being part of the political process. Well, I'll tell you what. That whole time we were being so careful and diplomatic, Caiaphas and Company were plotting His death. They read our sympathies and shut us out.

"Joseph, we were fools."

The men fell silent, watching. For the thousandth time, Nicodemus played in his memory the videotape of his one interview with Jesus.

He had been hearing amazing things about this Preacher from Galilee. Stories of exorcisms, healings, even resurrections. But more captivating than the miracles were the descriptions of the power of His preaching and of an indefinable aura of genuine, profound godliness. If even half was true, the Man deserved a careful hearing. Then, to cap it all, Jesus had turned up in Jerusalem and single-handedly emptied the temple court of livestock dealers and money lenders. The high priest and his comrades had been outraged; Nicodemus had secretly cheered.

Nicodemus had felt a professional obligation to familiarize himself with the work of Someone arousing this much interest among devout people. He was a much sought-after scholar and advisor. Among the Pharisees, he was known as "The Teacher." He felt the weight of people's confidence; he wasn't just another religious functionary. Nicodemus was a man of God. The supreme aim of his life was to obey the requirements of the Almighty and to help others do the same. How could he responsibly evaluate the new Teacher without some firsthand knowledge? People were constantly asking him what he thought.

And there was more, though he scarcely dared admit it, even to himself. The new Teacher evinced an intimacy with the Almighty that Nicodemus coveted.

Still, Nicodemus felt that his role required a certain discretion. It would not be proper to give the wrong impression to the masses. So he arranged an evening appointment.

Following his usual habit of gracious conversation, Nicodemus greeted the Teacher with strong affirmation. It was not insincere, but neither was it much more than courtesy. " 'Rabbi, we know that You are a teacher come from God; for no one can do these signs that You do unless God is with him' " (John 3:2, NKJV).

Jesus responded with unsettling directness: " 'Unless a person is born again, he cannot see the kingdom of God' " (verse 3, NKJV).

Nicodemus's mind reeled. Did Jesus actually mean that he, Nicodemus, needed to be born again? Or was He simply stating general spiritual truth? Was He attacking the Pharisees' emphasis on spiritual disciplines?

Nicodemus had responded with a rather inane question. He still colored a bit when he thought of it: "Surely a man cannot reenter the uterus and be born a second time!"

"No," Jesus had replied, "but the Spirit of God can accomplish something dramatic; it can bring about the birth of new spiritual life. The wind is invisible, but its power is unmistakable. That's also true of the Spirit. Its reality and power is demonstrated in the people who have been born again from above. I'm not just talking ideas. My ministry is about reality, about a change in the connection between people and heaven."

Jesus did not press him, but Jesus was offering him something he did not have—intimacy with the Almighty, a freshness and newness in life. Something that would come to him from God, not something he achieved himself through the disciplines of study, fasting, ritual purity, and correct worship practices.

But how does one start over? There were no bad habits Nicodemus could renounce. He was not like the prostitutes and mafiosos who found radically new lives through the teaching of Jesus. How does one repent of careful Sabbath keeping, disciplined purity, scrupulous tithing, and almost fanatical honesty? How does one experience newness in religious life when he has been living and teaching right doctrine, supporting the church with money and time, and upholding by word and example the standards of the people of God? Nicodemus was not playing games when he worshiped and prayed and studied the Scriptures. As a Pharisee, he carefully maintained the outward forms of piety, not for show, but as an integral part of his faith.

Nicodemus had not resolved his questions that evening with Jesus. He did not resolve them over the next three years of secret admiration.

Standing now, arms folded over his chest, staring at the three crosses, Nicodemus suddenly recalled Jesus' words at the end of their interview. "Remember, Nicodemus," He had said, gesturing upward with His index finger, "just as Moses lifted up the snake on a pole in the desert, in the same way, the Son of Man must be lifted up so the people who believe in Him can live."

Nicodemus knew what the rabbis said about this incident mentioned in the third book of Moses—almost nothing. They did not know what to do with it. The people of Israel on the long march from Egypt to Canaan had been complaining again. Finally God, in judgment, allowed desert vipers into the camp, and people started dying from snakebite. And as usual, they cried to Moses and God for relief.

But then the story takes a mysterious twist. For a remedy, God directed Moses to make a bronze sculpture of a snake and erect it on a pole. Anyone who looked at the metal serpent lived.

The Hebrew Scriptures were replete with symbolic representations of Messiah. He is called King of kings. He is pictured as the chief of all prophets, the highest high priest, and as the sun, rising and bringing healing. He was the Lion of the tribe of Judah, the Shepherd of Israel, the eagle hovering over its young. Many things that brought benefit to God's people spoke in some way of the mission of Messiah—the temple, the miracle food from heaven, the morning dawn. But a SERPENT? To the Jewish mind, a serpent spoke of uncleanness or evil. To think of Messiah as represented in the bronze snake was a difficult and startling thought.

All morning, ever since first hearing of the arrest and trial of Jesus, Nicodemus had been going over in his mind the prophecies about Messiah. How could he reconcile the grand images of Daniel with the images of suffering and death in Isaiah? Daniel writes that Messiah will rule the nations with a rod of iron. Isaiah says He will be slaughtered like a compliant sheep. How could He do both?

He remembered the reaction in the Sanhedrin last year when he protested their kangaroo court approach to Jesus. Nicodemus had blown the whole procedure out of the water by asking a simple question, "Does our law judge a man before it hears him and knows what he is doing?"

His comment infuriated the high priest, Caiaphas. Some of Caiaphas's allies on the council attacked him verbally and, in the process, referred to a Messianic prophecy. "Are you from the backwoods of Galilee too?" They asked sarcastically. "You know good and well that the Great Prophet will not come out of Galilee. Messiah will come from heaven, not from the sticks."

The Messiah was to come from heaven. He would rule with a rod of iron over Israel's enemies. Majesty, dignity, wealth, splendor would attend His reign. Isn't that what Nicodemus had believed too? . . . And taught for forty years?

Why was he standing here honoring a Man on a cross? Moses had written, "Cursed is everyone who hangs on a tree." The Messiah could *not* end His life on a cross. His place was on a throne. How could the Man nailed to those Roman boards be the King of the Jews?

Nicodemus's train of thought was interrupted by another.

What did he care anymore about Jerusalem and politics and respectability? If culture meant crucifying the best preacher and noblest Man Jerusalem had seen in his lifetime, then he *preferred* the backwoods. That Man dying on the middle cross had stirred his mind and his heart more than anything else in his whole life.

His mind jumped again. A snake on a pole. He had to admit the symbol did seem to fit Jesus now. The men on either side of Him really looked like snakes—poisonous men who certainly deserved death, if not crucifixion. So the One in the center might be looked upon as the king of thieves, the great snake.

Nicodemus remained on Golgotha through the afternoon. He saw the thief repent and heard Jesus respond with His trademark graciousness. Nicodemus was still there as a strange darkness engulfed the hill, terrifying and cowing the mocking crowd.

"So God has not gone to sleep or on vacation!" Nicodemus spoke in a low voice, half to himself, half to Joseph. "And our confidence in the Nazarene was not so wrong after all. Remember the words of the prophet." Good Pharisee that he was, Nicodemus knew the scripture by heart:

> The great day of the LORD is near . . .
> The mighty men shall cry out.
> That day *is* a day of wrath,
> A day of trouble and distress,
> A day of devastation and desolation,
> A day of darkness and gloominess,
> A day of clouds and thick darkness
> (Zephaniah 1:14, 15, NKJV).

"God's not pleased with what He's watching today."

Nicodemus smiled wryly. "But at least He's not blind. Nor is He helpless."

While others panicked, Nicodemus stood—solid as granite. He was too old to run from God's judgment. He felt he deserved it anyway for his cowardice. If this blackness was the chariot of the Judge, he would stand and meet it. He'd offer no excuses for his past timidity, but this time he'd stay with the Man on the cross, no matter what it cost him.

A little later when Jesus groaned His spine-chilling cry, "*Eloi, eloi, lama sabachthani,*" some thought He was calling for Elijah. Nicodemus knew better. He understood Jesus' Aramaic. In his mind echoed the words of the psalm, the first line of which Jesus had quoted:

> My God, My God, why have You forsaken Me?
> Why are You so far from helping Me,
> And from the words of My groaning?
> O My God, I cry in the daytime, but You do not
> hear
>   (Psalm 22:1, 2, NKJV).

Suddenly an entirely new perspective on Scripture began to open in Nicodemus's mind. The snake on the pole in the desert, the God-forsaken man of Psalm 22, the silent lamb of Isaiah who was counted with transgressors—maybe they were all the same. He did not yet know how to put it all together, but it was there.

Was today just the beginning of the day of the Lord? Was this dying as chief of thieves the necessary preparation for ruling with the rod of iron? Was this merely the first phase in a grand design for Messiah's triumph?

The snake was mounted on the pole because of the rebellion of God's people. But it brought healing. The servant of

God in Isaiah was wounded and bruised for the wrongs of God's people. But his punishment brought them peace.

Fresh shame invaded Nicodemus's mind. From the time of his interview with Jesus, Nicodemus had been awed by His power and teachings. But he had constantly fretted over Jesus' lack of credentials. One expects a teacher to possess certain formal measures of competence. Though he had never said so out loud, it bothered Nicodemus that Jesus' ministry was centered in backward, culturally deprived Galilee. Why hadn't He based His ministry in Jerusalem? Here, staring at the cross, Nicodemus realized how confined he'd been by the conventions of his own society. Even while he fought Caiaphas and other unscrupulous religious leaders, he had still lived in their world. He had measured Jesus with their yardstick.

The hours spent watching Jesus on the cross created a new yardstick. The cross broke Nicodemus's reserve. He yielded unreserved allegiance to Jesus of Nazareth, the King of the Jews.

Criminals sentenced to crucifixion were not supposed to be buried. They were discarded in the city dump. Joseph and Nicodemus were determined Jesus would have better. Late in the afternoon, they noticed the soldiers checking the men on the crosses. They cringed as the soldiers broke the thieves' legs to speed up their dying. When the soldiers checked Jesus, He was already dead. The centurion felt Jesus' leg for a pulse. Nothing. One of the soldiers jabbed Jesus with a spear just to make sure. No response.

Joseph and Nicodemus strode forward to the centurion. The officer responded to their greeting, noting their obvious status. "Yes," He confirmed, "Jesus is dead."

"We would appreciate it, sir, if you would not do anything with the body until we've had time to speak with Pilate."

"As you wish, gentlemen. If you like, I'll accompany you to

see him." The centurion was relieved. All afternoon he had been mentally suppressing the repeated evidences that Jesus of Nazareth was unique. Jesus' final cry and the earthquake had finally broken through his reservations and resistance. He was convinced this Man was no criminal; in fact, that He was more than human. What was the expression he had heard about Him? Son of God.

Hardened military man that he was, the centurion was reluctant to discard the body of a god in the garbage dump. But what choice did he have? He did not write the orders. He was grateful for the intervention of these obviously influential strangers.

Leaving Nicodemus at Golgotha, Joseph strode rapidly toward the city, accompanied by the Roman officer. At Pilate's palace, he was received promptly. When he asked for the body of Jesus so they could bury Him, Pilate was startled. He summoned the centurion from the entry hall to ask if it were really true that Jesus was dead. Then he granted Joseph the body.

Joseph and Nicodemus, aristocrats whose homes were full of servants, did not delegate the burial. At the cemetery, the two men personally prepared Jesus' body, using fabric and spices Nicodemus had bought. The spices—about a hundred pounds of myrrh and aloes—were fabulously expensive. Even so, Nicodemus considered them too small a statement of his admiration and sense of guilt. He was too late. He should have declared his friendship three years ago. Still, he thanked God his money could provide some dignity to the King in His death.

The tomb, a room carved in limestone exposed on the hillside, was a new one recently excavated for Joseph's family. It was closed by a huge rolling stone disk.

Nicodemus was right when he said God can use any fool. He and Joseph felt keenly the guilt of their timidity during the years of Jesus' ministry. But as foolish as they had been,

God did not reject them. Instead, now that they were willing to go public with their allegiance, God gave them a significant honor. To bury someone is the last act of love. To be allowed that was a mercy, a severe mercy to be sure, but genuine mercy still.

Jesus' closest associates and relatives—His mother, John, Peter, the women from Galilee who huddled in a group some distance from the cross—none of them could have buried Jesus. The government would not have released the body to them. And even if Jesus' friends could have obtained the body, they did not have the resources to do anything special. So God used Joseph and Nicodemus to provide a royal burial, giving dignity to Jesus and solace to His friends.

Joseph had been even more hesitant than Nicodemus to admit any sensibility to the nobility and authority of Jesus. He had been paralyzed by fear that the ruling clique in the Sanhedrin would discover his sympathies. But that afternoon of watching Jesus die had emboldened him. Heedless of agents of Caiaphas, he marched brazenly away from Golgotha with a Roman centurion beside him. He unhesitatingly strode right into Pilate's residence to ask for the body of Jesus, despite the bans against doing such a thing on Passover eve. In his meeting with Pilate he spoke with calm authority. His bold sympathy for Jesus gave the Roman procurator his first evidence that the Sanhedrin was not united in its verdict against Jesus of Nazareth.

Nicodemus, too, was transformed that afternoon in the presence of Jesus. There on Golgotha his knowledge of the prophecies, his memory of Jesus' words in their interview, and the sight of Jesus hung up against the sky—all came together and overwhelmed his reserve. He gave himself unreservedly to Jesus. His heart was broken as he helped to close the tomb. But he went home with the small comfort that, however late, he had stood for Jesus. He had finally done what he could.

It is God's way to use the weight of our greatest failures to pull us down into His grace so that we might find new life. So it was with Nicodemus. In the years after Jesus' crucifixion, looking back at that blackest of all days, Nicodemus would realize it was actually his birthday—the day he was born again.

ABANDONED!
MY GOD, WHY HAVE YOU FORSAKEN ME?

"My God, my God, why have you forsaken me?" These must be some of the most mysterious words Jesus ever spoke.

They are reported by both Matthew and Mark. Matthew wrote for a Jewish audience and aimed to show that Jesus was the fulfillment of the Old Testament prophecies pointing forward to a Messiah. Mark wrote for a Roman audience and aimed to show Jesus' Lordship through His vigorous action and bold leadership. Both Jewish and Roman audiences would have found these words of Jesus perplexing, alien, utterly incomprehensible.

It seems to me we are no less offended today. What could Jesus have possibly meant?

The answer can be stated simply, though it stretches our minds to understand it. These words were not mere drama for drama's sake; they expressed the reality of what Jesus was experiencing. He endured abandonment by God. Jesus, on the cross, so identified Himself with sinners that He endured the separation from God, which is the natural, inevitable consequence of doing wrong.

One of the surprising elements of Jesus' ministry was the

intensity of His identification with sinners.

At the very beginning of His ministry, Jesus was baptized. Baptism was a sign of confession of sin. "John came, baptizing in the desert region and preaching a baptism of repentance for the forgiveness of sins." Thousands went out to hear Him. "Confessing their sins, they were baptized" (Mark 1:4, 5). But Jesus had no sin of His own to confess. Still He was baptized. And by requesting baptism, He declared His solidarity with sinners.

Throughout His ministry, Jesus deliberately took on Himself the shame and ostracism of people unfit for polite and godly society. He fraternized with a Samaritan woman, violating Jewish taboos against social interaction with an apostate, a woman, and an adulteress. He took on Himself the condemnation attached to her.

Probably no group in Jewish society was as despised as the tax collectors who worked for Rome. Regarded as quislings, as traitors, they had the moral and social status of drug dealers in mainstream America. They were hated. Jesus not only called a tax collector, Matthew, to serve in His inner circle, but when Matthew held a banquet for all his unreconstructed associates, Jesus attended as guest of honor. Matthew and his friends were delighted; the religious leaders were scandalized.

Lepers were regarded as suffering under the curse of God. They were absolutely untouchable. Some rabbis even boasted that they threw stones at lepers whenever they saw them to make sure they didn't approach too closely. In Jesus' first recorded encounter with a leper in the Gospel of Matthew, the very first thing He does is reach out His hand and touch the untouchable. Jesus entered the leper's world, taking on Himself the leper's uncleanness, his pariah status, before healing him.

Then there is the wonderful story of Mary Magdalene (see

chapter 10). Her history included demon possession and gross sexual immorality. She came into the banquet room, poured pricy perfume over Jesus, then knelt at His feet, kissing them and wiping her tears from them with her hair. This would have been utterly scandalous behavior by any woman, let alone someone with Mary's background. But Jesus not only refused to reprove her, He commended her and chided those who criticized her lavish expenditure and her forwardness.

Jesus took on Himself her shame. In the eyes of His critics, He sank to her level. In the eyes of Mary and the Christian church, Jesus raised her into His world.

On Golgotha as a final symbol of his identification with sinners, Jesus was crucified between two thieves. Isaiah, the prophet, had written five hundred years earlier, "He willingly gave his life and shared the fate of evil men" (Isaiah 53:12, TEV). On the cross between two thieves, Jesus looked like the king of thieves.

Jesus not only modeled identification with sinners, He explicitly declared that such identification was central to the meaning of His ministry.

Perhaps the most dramatic statement of Jesus' union with sinners came in a conversation He had with Nicodemus. In describing His own work, Jesus said,

> As Moses lifted up the bronze snake on a pole in the desert, in the same way the Son of Man must be lifted up, so that everyone who believes in him may have eternal life (John 3:14-16, TEV).

Nicodemus was shocked by Jesus' words. In the Hebrew Scriptures, the snake represented the devil! How could a snake illustrate the work of Jesus, the sinless Son of God? The solution to the riddle is stated explicitly by the apostle Paul: "God made him who had no sin to be sin for us, so that in him we might become the righteousness of God" (2 Corinthians 5:21). On the cross as He hung dying, Jesus so identified Himself with the sins of humanity that He could appropriately claim for Himself the devil's sign—a snake.

On the cross Jesus actually accepted the wrath of God deserved by sinners. Isaiah described His suffering this way, "All of us were like sheep that were lost, each of us going his own way. But the Lord made the punishment fall on him, the punishment all of us deserved" (Isaiah 53:6, TEV). That punishment included separation from God the Father. "Your iniquities have separated you from your God; your sins have hidden his face from you . . ." (Isaiah 59:2).

When Jesus cried out, "My God, my God, why have you forsaken me?" He was not playacting. He was expressing the searing reality of separation from God.

The apostle John writes that Jesus was the "propitiation for our sins, and not for ours only but also for the whole world" (1 John 2:2, NKJV). To propitiate means to "conciliate an offended power." God is the guarantor of justice in the universe. He cannot ignore cruelty, malevolence, treachery, sin.

Sin is self-destructive. But it is much more than that. It is "other-destructive." It harms God's other children, sullies His world, and defames His character. Because of the deadly impact of our sinful actions, we deserve death. Propitiation refers to some action that turns God's wrath away from the sinner.

The word *propitiation* is often thought of in pagan terms: A human effort to appease an offended God. The uniquely Christian understanding of this word is that the members of the Godhead provided what was required to satisfy justice and to restore moral equilibrium in the universe. Through the death of Jesus, the Godhead provided a way to maintain His inflexible and just hostility toward wrongdoing while extending mercy to wrongdoers. Jesus was the Godhead's representative when He died in our place. As a result, God is free to pardon us without the slightest risk of appearing to condone or even excuse wrongdoing. While God takes great delight in saving sinners, the cross is incontrovertible proof that He's not soft on injustice and evil.

The cross was not humanity's gift to God; it was not a desperate human effort to placate an enraged God. It was God's gift of peace to people incapable of coming to peace. The cross was not a statement of humanity's pursuit of God; it was a fantastic achievement in the divine pursuit of humanity.

When Jesus cried, "My God, my God, why have you forsaken me?" He did not just create a picture of divine love, though there is no greater demonstration. Because of His love, He actually altered the moral condition of the universe. He balanced the moral scales. He counteracted the chaotic inertia created by sin.

God does not simply excuse the sins of those He forgives; He makes Himself responsible for those sins. Instead of dismissing our moral debts as trivial, He Himself pays them. In the judgment, God will point to the cross as His answer to the question: What right do you have to pardon sinners?

This means that once we've confessed our sins and accepted forgiveness, we can resist the feeling that we must somehow atone for our sins. Certainly wherever it is at all possible, believers will make restitution for things they have wrongfully taken from others, whether tangible or intangible. They will work for reconciliation with people they have hurt. But balancing the cosmic scales, restoring harmony in a universe disordered by our sin has already been done. The blood-debt (described so vividly in the Old Testament) created by our wrongdoing has been paid by Jesus Christ. And we are now invited to rest in Jesus' accomplishment.

The modern mind is no less offended today by Jesus' cry than were first-century Jews, Romans, and Greeks. Surely, God is too nice to actually cause someone to die for sins. It cannot really be true that wrongdoing inevitably brings lethal consequences. Mild evil is surely excusable. The idea that God the Father would, in fact, separate Himself from Jesus as the essential divine antidote to the deadly effects of sin is just too barbarous to imagine.

But we have an intuitive logic that enables us to understand what God the Father and God the Son were doing. When we hear of someone embezzling millions of dollars from a bank or the stock exchange, we instinctively feel that whatever else happens, the embezzler ought to make restitution. This is the only way to really make it right. Unfortunately, often in real life, the crook has already spent most of the money; he lacks the resources to repay what he has stolen.

We are outraged when some high-powered crook avoids repaying his debts because of his social and political connections. And if a governor wishes to pardon an embezzler, then the governor should pay back the stolen dollars. We feel wronged when a swindler or embezzler gets off "scot-free."

At minimum, our sins are like moral embezzling. We have diverted our energy and intellect from honoring God and serving people to selfish objectives. We have stolen from God. We have robbed people around us. We ought to repay, but we can't. Jesus' death was God's way of paying off our debt to Himself and to the world.

Besides the fantastic truth that on the cross Jesus endured the punishment earned by all of us sinners, Jesus' words, "My God, my God, why have you forsaken me?" speak directly to the situation of some of His most troubled children.

Many Christians, including believers famous for their exemplary lives and effectiveness in preaching the gospel, have endured what is called "the dark night of the soul." These black nights are times when God seems to be unreachably distant or even hostile. The believer feels absolutely cut off from God, hopeless, and abandoned. To say it as it really feels: The Christian agonizing in the blackness of spiritual depression feels hopelessly damned.

The sufferer endlessly asks himself and God, "What did I do wrong? Where did I miss God's guidance for my life? What unknown sin am I indulging that is making God angry at me?"

No answers come. And the person feels utterly alone, isolated in the darkness. At these times Jesus invites you to remember His words, "My God, my God, why have you forsaken me?" Jesus knows how you feel. Despite His flawless morality and His privileges as the Son of God, Jesus knows by experience what it means to walk in darkness and see "no light" (Isaiah 50:10). He keeps company with you in your darkness.

It is not just spiritual depression that is brightened by Jesus' experience on the cross. His taste of darkness and estrangement makes Him the perfect friend to hang onto whenever your mind is overwhelmed or deranged by forces beyond your control.

You may be crippled by depression, perhaps even hospitalized. The darkness may seem unrelenting. Jesus has not forsaken you. You may be losing your mind through schizophrenia or Alzheimer's disease or some rare malfunction of the brain. As you feel yourself losing touch with reality, Jesus offers you His words as a prayer. "My God, my God, why have you forsaken me?"

It is not "unChristian" to find your mind swamped in blackness and despair. Jesus has been there too. So hang on to Jesus' words as your anchor, "My God, why have you forsaken me?"

And if you can, call to mind His other words, the very last message He gave to His disciples: "And surely I will be with you always, to the very end of the age" (Matthew 28:20). Remember His promise in Hebrews 13:5 (NKJV), " 'I will never leave you nor forsake you.' "

Jesus' experience of abandonment is the believer's greatest guarantee that God will never abandon us. We may feel God-forsaken, but if we throw ourselves on the mercy of God, we can be absolutely positive that, in fact, we are kept by His love. God is not going to waste the agony He endured at the cross by letting you go, despite your repentance. The only way He will let go of you is if you insist on it. And even then He will not easily let you go. He's invested too much.

Mary Magdalene

While he was in Bethany, reclining at the table in the home of a man known as Simon the Leper, a woman came with an alabaster jar of very expensive perfume, made of spikenard. She broke the jar and poured the perfume on his head (Mark 14:3, paraphrase).

And many women who followed Jesus from Galilee, ministering to Him, were there looking on from afar, among whom were Mary Magdalene, Mary the mother of James and Joses, and the mother of Zebedee's sons (Matthew 27:55, 56, NKJV).

In the motley audience on Golgotha, Mary alone had reason for joy. It wasn't much, but it was real.

The priests and the rabble laughed and joked. But their levity wasn't joy. The soldiers found diversion in their conversations; this was just a job to them. But callous indifference is hardly joy.

John was there, and probably the other disciples as well,

disappointed with themselves and their failures of the night before. Dazed by the tragedy.

Mary hurt as John did, maybe worse. Jesus had been everything to her. When He found her, she was in hell—literally possessed by demons, frequently abused by men. Jesus changed all that. He had set her free from the demons, seven times invading the devil's territory to rescue her.

Now He was dying. Who would protect her from demons and scheming men? Who would rescue her if she was entrapped? Who would save her from her own self-destructive urges? Whom would she live for? Whom would she love?

But unlike anyone else on Golgotha, in the midst of her bewildered grief, Mary had one little reason for joy. She remembered the feast at Simon's house.

It was a dinner to honor Jesus. Simon owed it. Jesus had healed him of leprosy.

Simon had tasted only the beginnings of the horrors of leprosy. He hadn't yet endured the creeping disfigurement, the loss of toes or fingers, nose or eyes. But he'd been quarantined, separated for life from his friends at the synagogue, prohibited by law from ever again participating in their worship or their debates over the Torah. He'd been completely cut off from any physical contact with his wife and children.

When you had leprosy, it was as though death already ate at your body even while you lived. It was the curse of God; it was here-and-now damnation.

The dinner was formal—black suit, black tie, cummerbund, and all the rest. Martha did her usual unexcelled job of catering. Elegance and protocol were flawless. Jesus and His inner circle ringed the table along with friends of Simon. Lazarus—good, faithful Lazarus—was there. He'd become something of a celebrity since his resurrection.

Mary knew what she was going to do was inappropriate.

People like her did not converse with or touch people like Jesus. But she had spent so much of her life being inappropriate she was used to it. She had saved and planned for buying this perfume. She knew some of her friends would tease her about wasting a year's wages on a holy Man. She was only sorry she had no more to spend. Jesus was worth everything she had and more. Why did she pick this party? Why this afternoon? She didn't know. Something inside said, "Now!"

She had slipped in surreptitiously, broken the seal, and poured the perfume on Jesus' head. Then overcome with emotion, she fell at His feet crying silently. She kissed His feet and wiped the tears from them with her waist-length hair.

She could still feel the terror of the nights when the demons would assert their control. Too awful to recall voluntarily was the memory of mornings-after-the-nights-before of promiscuous sex. Hard men and unfriendly supernatural beings had controlled her life—used her, abused her, ruined her. Then this Man saved her. Exorcized the demons. Even when she appeared not to want deliverance. Then when He had made her His own by snatching her away from the demons and johns, instead of claiming His share of her favors, He gave her back her purity and set her free.

No wonder she cried.

Perfume is hard to hide. As the fragrance drifted around the room, Judas spoke up. He was quick. He had noticed Mary crying over Jesus' feet. He knew her story. It was a rather sorry one. Mary was one of the women who followed Jesus down from Galilee. She was the kind of person who gave their organization a bad name. Talk about riffraff. Her kind thought the sun rose and set in Jesus. They had no understanding of the kind of handling and maneuvering required to promote someone like Jesus. They had no appreciation for the skills of someone like Judas.

His annoyance finally erupted. "This is awful; it's downright sickening. Why wasn't this perfume sold and the money used to feed poor folk? You all know how important careful management of our resources is. A lot of people depend on us." To himself he fumed, "How can anyone justify spending that much money on perfume for Jesus? And this kissing and crying—it is disgusting. Does Jesus have no sense of propriety?"

Mary was shattered by Judas's words. She could hear the murmur of agreement around the table. She felt the old terror welling up inside; men, important men, disapproved of her. She had only meant to tell Jesus how much He had done for her. Had she made a mistake? Had she embarrassed Him? Had she wasted money Jesus would have preferred used some other way? Was it selfish to spend so much on a gift just for Him?

She glanced furtively at Simon. She could see the disgust on his face. He agreed with Judas. She had no right to touch the teacher. She wished that the floor would open and swallow her or that the roof would cave in. She cowered, clinging to the feet of the only man who had ever been able to rescue her.

Again Jesus breaks the power of those who would control her. "Leave her alone. Why do you trouble her? She has done a good work for me. You always have the poor with you, and whenever you wish, you may do them good. You will not always have Me with you. She has done what she could. She has come beforehand to anoint My body for burial."

There on Golgotha on Friday afternoon, mixed in with the stupefying hurt caused by Jesus' death, was the sweet memory of the perfume and His words, "She has done a good work for me." The rich melody of those words played over and over in her mind: "She has done a good work for me."

She had done it in time. She had done right. He said so. He

knew she owed Him everything—her life, her dignity, her womanhood. She had told Him, before He died. And now, even through her tears, she gave thanks she hadn't waited.

She hoped that there on the cross He remembered the perfume. She hoped He remembered her tears and kisses and would know there was at least one person in the world who knew how valuable His life had been. No matter what happened that afternoon on the hill, He would know He had saved one person. And to think she almost had not done it.

She remembered Simon's muttered complaint to Judas, "If Jesus knew what kind of woman that is, He would not allow her to touch Him. That much I know for sure."

Mary laughed to think about it now. It offered a bit of comic relief. *If Jesus had known what kind of woman were touching Him?* Why, Jesus knew more about her than Simon ever did. Besides, Simon wasn't all that pure himself, the hypocrite. She could tell a story or two.

Why did Simon think she was touching Him anyway? Did he, in his wildest dreams, think that she put Jesus in the same category as Simon? No way! Jesus was not another lover, not another customer. He was her Saviour. He had rescued her and remade her. She wasn't the kind of woman Simon thought she was. She had been, true enough. But this Man's touch had changed all that.

Perhaps the most amazing turn of the afternoon had been Jesus' reaction to Simon's mutterings. "Simon," he said, "I have a question." You could see Simon's face go white. He must have thought Jesus was going to expose him.

"A rich man had two aides. One owed him a hundred thousand dollars. The other servant owed him three hundred dollars. The rich man took pity on both of them and forgave their debts. Which one do you think loved the rich man more?"

Simon exhaled slowly through pursed lips. "I suppose the

one who was forgiven more."

"Right you are." Jesus responded. "You see this woman? When I came here, you didn't give me water to wash my feet, but she has washed them with tears and dried them with her hair. You didn't offer me any cologne; she has perfumed my head and my feet.

"Her sins were obvious and many. That's true. But the warmth and determination of her love just as obviously declare she has received full pardon for her sins."

Then turning to Mary, He said gently but loud enough that no one in the room missed His words, "Your sins are forgiven. You may go now in peace."

She left as in a dream. A queen dismissed to her palace.

Then this morning she heard He'd been arrested. She knew it couldn't be true. But it was. Then they had brought Him out here and nailed Him to a cross. She had never hurt this much in her life. But at least she had told Him in time.

Standing there, she could make no sense out of the day's happenings. The noblest, strongest Man who had ever lived was being executed as a usurper and traitor. To people who did not know Him, He appeared no different from the vermin on either side of Him. When she heard His sorrowful cry, "My God, my God, why have you forsaken me?" she echoed Him: "Yes, God, why have You forsaken Him? How could You do this? How could You forsake *us?*"

All Mary saw that afternoon was the triumph of evil. But in the future, when in memory she again stood and watched the Teacher suffer, she would understand it better than almost anyone else. She understood extravagant love. In her extravagant response to what Jesus had done for her, she had developed an intuitive understanding of *God's* love. Her own experience of giving everything was a finger play of the Trinity's decision to spend the resources of heaven to ransom sinful humans from their self-inflicted slavery.

There are three sermons in Mary's story: Do it. Do it richly. Do it now.

Too often we bemoan our imagined poverty, saying, "If only I had a million dollars, I'd build a new science building at our church's college. I would buy motorcycles for the pastors in Africa who serve twenty or thirty churches, traveling between them on foot because they cannot afford a bicycle or bus tickets. Or, I would see to it that quality Christian programming was on the air in every city in the country. If only I could preach like Billy Graham or H. M. S. Richards; if only I could teach with the skill of Brother Jackson; then I could really do something for God."

Surrounded by opportunities to encourage with a letter or phone call, we do nothing. In practically every church there are single folks and lonely couples we could invite for lunch. Everywhere—at work, next door, at school, at church—there are people we could love. We could help. Instead, we daydream of doing something great.

Mary could not preach like Peter. She could not command the lame to stand and walk. She couldn't travel as a missionary to Turkey and Greece. But she did what she could. She didn't wait to be asked. She did not require recognition or official sanction; she simply found a way to love. Mary did what she could with what she had. We need to quit dreaming and do it.

Mary loved richly. She was reckless and extravagant in love. Many husbands need to learn from her. We need to consider the need of our wives for "nice" things. Frugality is a virtue, but sometimes it is merely a front for stinginess. For some husbands, opening the checkbook would be an appropriate and powerful expression of affection. Love, by its very nature, is occasionally extravagant.

By some "objective measures," it's a waste of money to buy

flowers and perfume, to give spikenard. But by His acceptance of Mary's fragrant gift of love, Jesus showed there are times when it is most appropriate.

Husbands and wives need to spend time and money on each other within reasonable limits. Maybe it could mean long-stem red roses for your wife, accompanied by your hug. Maybe candlelight dinners now and then. Possibly you could surprise your husband with a special dish when you know he's not expecting it. Go the extra mile. Give of yourself. Jesus dignified generous expressions of love by His affirmation of Mary's gift.

This same principle applies to all our relationships. Friends, coworkers, parents and children, teachers and students, pastors and parishioners, employers and employees—all need the sweetness of expressed appreciation.

Mary, no doubt, never again had the kind of money she spent on that perfume, but she never regretted her love-gift to Jesus. We, too, will treasure the memories of the "extravagances" that express our love. Let's love richly.

Do it now. Mary's perfume brought far more joy to Jesus than the lavish funeral arrangements Nicodemus provided. One rose now is worth more than a hundred on a casket. Some of the saddest times in my pastoral work have been listening to sobs of people bitterly regretting their failure to say I love you or Thank you in time. They had always meant to do it; they just never got around to it. Suddenly it was too late. Eulogies are not heard by the person eulogized.

Mary gave her perfume and kisses in time. Let's do the same.

Jesus had been the focus of attention for thousands. Five thousand plus people had hung on His every word then eaten a supper He miraculously created. On another occasion, four thousand plus did the same. He had nearly been pushed into the lake by a crowd of eager listeners. Once while He was preaching in a house, Jesus had been interrupted by four men making a hole in the roof. They were attempting to get their friend to Jesus so He could heal him. The crowd around the house had been that thick.

On the cross Jesus was alone. Some of his friends stood at a distance, displaced from their rightful place near the cross by the hostile rabble. John, Jesus' mother, and Mary Magdalene had pushed through the mob to the foot of the cross. But when John and Jesus' mother left, Mary stayed. She was still there when He cried out because He felt God had abandoned Him—her perfume, she hoped, vivid in His memory, her presence His only apparent support.

Jesus had told Simon that the greatest debtor, once forgiven, becomes the greatest lover. Mary would claim her place as one of these. She had anointed Him ahead of time for His burial; she would stay to the end. Of all the friends of Jesus, Mary is the only one mentioned by name that we know for sure was there when He died. That is a hard privilege, but a privilege nonetheless. She was there when they took Him down from the cross. She followed Him to the grave site. She saw Him interred. She was first at the grave on Sunday morning.

And Jesus honored Mary's tenacious love.

On Friday, Mary's world collapsed. All that was left to give purpose to her life was to grieve His memory. But when she went to the grave on Sunday morning, bringing more perfume, she found that someone had opened the grave and taken His body! Had the owner of the grave changed His mind and ordered the body removed? Had the authorities decided after all that Jesus couldn't be buried in a proper cemetery?

Nearly hysterical, she ran back to Jerusalem and told the rest of the disciples. Peter and John raced off toward the tomb, and she followed them back to the tomb. Eventually they left. Finally Mary, too, walked away from the grave nearly incoherent with grief. Almost immediately she stumbled blindly into a man who asked sympathetically, "Why are you crying? Who are you looking for?"

Taking Him to be a gardener, she mumbled, "Excuse me, sir, do you know where they have taken Him? If you had to take Him out of here, can't you tell me where you put Him? I'll take care of Him." She stares unseeing at the ground, waiting.

The entire population of heaven is waiting for His answer. Angels are waiting to take Jesus back to heaven to greet the Father. The agony of the weekend is over. The suspense of the past thirty-three years is over, and Jesus has won. Hundreds of thousands of angels line the approaches to the throne. The Father Himself stands with eager expectancy to receive His Son.

But the King of the Universe waited. The angels waited. The universe waited . . . for the Son to greet Mary.

The supposed gardener finally spoke. "Mary."

His voice penetrates her grief-induced, mental haze. "Teacher!" She throws herself at His feet and grips them, crying, "You're alive!"

"Don't hold me, Mary." Jesus said quietly. "I have not yet gone to greet my Father. I need you to do something for me. Go, tell My brothers, Peter and John and the others, that I am returning to My Father and your Father, to My God and your God. Go now." He put His hand on her head, gently pulled His feet from her grasp and was gone.

Again she had reason to live. She had a job to do and, because He lived, courage to do it.

I'm Thirsty!

After this, Jesus, knowing that everything was now completed, so that the Scripture might be fulfilled, said, "I am thirsty." A vessel full of sour wine was there, so they soaked a sponge in the wine, put the sponge on a stalk of hyssop and lifted it to his mouth (John 19:28, 29, paraphrase).

Then the King will say to those on His right hand, "Come, you blessed of My Father, inherit the kingdom prepared for you from the foundation of the world: for . . . I was thirsty and you gave Me drink" (Matthew 25:34-40, NKJV).

God uses some strange disguises. He meets us in the most surprising places. Can you imagine a divine Being actually calling out, "I am thirsty"?

God is not supposed to be dependent on humans:

"If I were hungry, I would not tell you;
For the world is Mine, and all its fullness"

(Psalm 50:12, NKJV).

Jesus was divine. Even while on earth He had full access to the powers of the Godhead, and He used that power freely in His ministry. On at least two occasions He created food for thousands, starting from almost nothing (Matthew 14:13-21; 15:29-39). He transformed water into grape juice (John 2:1-11). When Peter got caught in an argument about a tax payment, Jesus saved him from embarrassment by directing him to catch a fish and pay the tax with the coin he would find in the fish's mouth! (Matthew 17:24-27). Despite all this, on the cross He was helpless. By choice.

Jesus' life was filled with miracles. But He did not work miracles for Himself. All that divine power was concentrated on other people. Jesus didn't make food for himself. He didn't make wine for Himself. He didn't calm storms for Himself. He performed all these astounding miracles for others. He refused to use His divine power to fill His own personal needs.

So when Jesus got thirsty while He was hanging on the cross, He needed someone else to get him a drink.

One of the special agonies of crucifixion was thirst. And in Jesus' case, His thirst was exacerbated by the blood loss during the floggings. He had refused the offer of some bitter wine shortly after arriving on Golgotha. He wanted to keep His mind clear for His war with the devil and His ministry to the thief and Mary and John and the soldiers. Now He was finished. He had defeated the devil; He had secured salvation for humanity; He had spoken the gospel to the thief. He was ready to rest. After hours of fighting an unspeakably wrenching spiritual battle, He finally paid attention to His body. Every cell was craving water. His tongue was thick, His lips cracked. He croaked, "I am thirsty."

The King of the universe, Almighty-God-in-the-Flesh,

needed somebody to give Him a drink.

The biblical context of these words gives them added punch. They come near the end of the Gospel of John, famous for its theological discourse and its elegant passages on spiritual life. Jesus' cry "I'm thirsty" coming at the end of this profound theological book reminds us that real theology is not pie-in-the-sky theory. It's not a collection of abstract ideas and complicated words. Theology is discourse about God. And real theology leads inescapably to concrete, compassionate action.

Jesus was a real human being. He was unique in that from conception He was "the holy one" and the "Son of God" (Luke 1:35). He was unique in that half His genetic heritage was absolutely perfect, created by the Holy Spirit. But He was made "like his brothers in every way" (Hebrews 2:17, NIV). "He himself suffered when he was tempted" (Hebrews 2:18, NIV). He was tempted in every way, just as we are (Hebrews 4:15). Perhaps most surprising of all, "he learned obedience in the school of suffering" (Hebrews 5:8, NEB).

Matthew wrote that Jesus would be called Immanuel, which means " 'God is with us' " (Matthew 1:23, TEV). There are two foci in this sentence; both are significant: 1. Jesus was really God. 2. Jesus was truly one of us; He was human.

The gospels recount many evidences of His genuine humanity. While traveling in Samaria, He got tired and thirsty and asked a stranger for some water (John 4:6,7). He got sleepy, and He upset His disciples by sleeping during a violent storm that nearly sank their boat (Mark 4:35-41). He enjoyed good food and good drink (Matthew 11:19).

He responded to human kindness (Matthew 26:10-13). He needed His friends when He was under stress and was disappointed when they let Him down (Matthew 26:36-40). He had special friends (John 11:3). He was a real man.

The cry from the cross, "I am thirsty," was a final dramatic expression of His humanity. He needed someone to give Him a drink. He would not use His divine power to cause a waterpot to miraculously appear midair and tip itself up so He could have a swallow. Jesus called for human help.

The Son of God needed an ordinary human being to do Him a favor.

This scene at the cross drives home the message of the most famous judgment passage in the New Testament:

> Then the King will say to those on his right, "Come, you who are blessed by my Father; take your inheritance, the kingdom prepared for you since the creation of the world. For I was hungry and you gave me something to eat, I was thirsty and you gave me something to drink, I was a stranger and you invited me in, I needed clothes and you clothed me, I was sick and you looked after me, I was in prison and you came to visit me (Matthew 25:34-36, NIV).

The people are astonished at the Judge's words. When did we ever see you thirsty and give you a drink, they want to know. His answer, of course: Whatever you did for one of the least of these brothers of mine, you did for me.

Every time you meet a concrete, genuine human need, you're serving Jesus.

Jesus, who was truly God, experienced genuine human need, which could be filled by other human beings. And in the crying need of people around us, Jesus wants us to hear His voice.

When you struggle out of bed at three in the morning to take care of a sick baby for the fifth time since midnight, that is the same as caring for Jesus. When you help ease the burden a single mother carries, you are easing Jesus' burden. When you invest time and money in prison ministry, you're investing in Jesus. When you sacrifice some luxury so you can give more to a clean water project in Cambodia, you are giving to Jesus.

The Bible constantly urges action to ease human need. The prophet Isaiah rebukes Israel for thinking they could substitute formal religious practices for down-to-earth kindness. He quotes God:

> "Is not this the kind of [religion] I have chosen: . . .
> Is it not to share your food with the hungry
> and to provide the poor wanderer with shelter—
> when you see the naked, to clothe him,
> and not to turn away from your own flesh and
> blood?"
> (Isaiah 58:6, 7 NIV).

Other well-known passages are:

> He who is kind to the poor lends to the LORD, and he will reward him for what he has done (Proverbs 19:17, NIV).

> What God the Father considers to be pure and genuine religion is this: to take care of orphans and widows in their suffering and to keep oneself from being corrupted by the world (James 1:27, TEV).

> My children, our love should not be just words and talk; it must be true love, which shows itself in action" (1 John 3:18, TEV).

One of the strongest affirmations Jesus gave anyone during His ministry was to Mary Magdalene: " 'She has done a beautiful thing to me. . . . I tell you the truth, wherever the gospel is preached throughout the world, what she has done will also be told, in memory of her' " (Mark 14:6, 9, NIV). What did she do to earn such praise? It wasn't preaching or miracle working or martyrdom. Jesus honored her for an act of personal affection. She poured expensive perfume on Him.

If we're looking for Jesus' approval, we will copy Mary in giving personal attention to people. Any kindness done in Jesus' name will be honored as though it were done personally to Him.

Sarah Pollack's parents promised her a car for graduation—if she earned good grades and a college scholarship.

Well, Sarah lived up to her end of the bargain. She got straight A's and a $5,000 scholarship. But instead of enjoying a new car as a well-earned reward, she took her parents' gift of $15,000 and started a college fund to help needy students.

When asked why she did it, she replied, "I heard so many horror stories from my classmates about their mad scramble to pay bills that I wanted to do something. They were friends. They were people I respected, with talent. It really just killed me that they could go nowhere" (Youth Worker Update, September 1995, 4).

When you think of the millions of young people around the world who need assistance with getting an education, Sarah's $15,000 isn't much. She could have easily reasoned that the need was so great, even in her own town, that she couldn't make any real difference. But instead of thinking like that, Sarah Pollack did what she could.

Children, neighbors, and feeble senior citizens; husbands, wives and perfect strangers; pastors, Sabbath School teachers, and long-time backsliders—all of them represent Jesus to us if they have a need we can fill. Baby-sitting, gifts of money, fixing a lawn mower, an anonymous card saying Thank you, a weekly ride to the grocery store—the needs are endless. Mary did what she could. God calls us to do the same.

When Jesus called out "I'm thirsty," someone, probably a soldier, soaked a sponge in some wine vinegar, put the sponge on a stick, and lifted it to Jesus' mouth. The soldier was certainly unaware that he was doing noteworthy service. He did not expect to have his action recorded in a history that would still be widely read two thousand years later. He did what needed to be done. He gave the man a drink. He served the Son of God.

Jesus spent His life serving others. He employed all the power of heaven to ease human suffering. He miraculously fed people. He healed every conceivable affliction—incurable diseases, demonic possession, epilepsy, physical deformity, congenital blindness. Through His preaching He gave new life to thousands in His day and created a new understanding of God, which has continued to transform lives for two thousand years. But even as the divine Son of God, He relied on others to help Him.

He borrowed Peter's boat to use as a pulpit. Another time He had His disciples keep a boat ready for Him in case the press of the crowd became too much and He had to escape (Mark 4:1; 3:9). He preached in synagogues when others invited Him (Luke 4:14-17). He accepted money to support His entourage, and women traveled with His company, helping to the ministry financially and serving Him (John 12:6; Luke 8:1-3; Matthew 27:55).

At the beginning of His final week of ministry, when He rode into Jerusalem like a king surrounded by cheering crowds, He was riding a borrowed donkey (Matthew 21:1-3). He relied on an anonymous benefactor for the room where He shared the Last Supper with His disciples (Matthew 26:18,19). On Friday, when Jesus was struggling to get His cross to Golgotha where He would accomplish the expiation of the sins of the entire human race, He needed a stranger's help to get His cross to the top of the hill (Matthew 27:32).

Jesus still relies on helpers to accomplish His work. He invites us to be part of His ministry. He gives us the honor of representing Him and making a difference in people's lives by passing on to them His love.

We are surrounded by calls for help. Often, it seems as though our help will not make much difference. The big problems of the world remain no matter what we do. But we can do something for the person close to us. We can bring flowers to our wives. We can tell our children "I love you." We can help out in the children's program at church. We can offer encouragement to a coworker. We can say Thank you to someone who thinks they're just doing a job. We cannot heal the world, but we can love someone. And we must.

Jesus is thirsty, and He asks us to give Him a drink in the person of His children. Jesus would have us hear, in the plight of people who need our help, His own voice crying from the cross, "I am thirsty."

Retraining the Thunder:
John, Part One

Ye know not what spirit ye are of (Luke 9:55, KJV).

In A.D. 342, there were terrible riots in Constantinople. Three thousand people lost their lives. Some of the worst bloodshed occurred in the streets in front of churches. The people who were killed were Christians. The killers, too, called themselves Christians.

What were they fighting for? Why were they attacking and butchering each other? The honor of Jesus. They were fighting over different beliefs about the nature of Christ.

Violence in the name of Christ. It's probably the greatest scandal in the entire history of Christianity. During the troubles in Northern Ireland, Catholics and Protestants both have considered themselves Christians. And for years extremists in both groups have used bombs and bullets against those they disagreed with.

In Bosnia, the Orthodox Serbs and Roman Catholic Croats have used their religious differences as part of their justification for unrelenting warfare. In fact, some observers say that the conflict in Bosnia is almost exclusively religious. A Serb who becomes a Catholic is regarded as a Croat. And vice versa.

In the first part of this decade in southern Mexico, mobs led by Catholic priests attacked evangelical Christians—in the name of Christ.

How should we respond when the honor of Christ is insulted, when the honor of Christianity is dragged in the dirt by someone else? For the disciple John, the cross was a graduate course in how to respond to indignity. Christ's willingness to allow Himself to be crucified was the ultimate lesson in a three-year education.

From childhood John had considered it a matter of integrity and justice for a man to defend his honor with his fists. Fighting was in his blood. Jesus called John and his brother, James, the Sons of Thunder because of their explosive tempers. If there was one positive trait that John excelled in, it was loyalty. He was fiercely loyal to Jesus. He was hypersensitive to the honor of Jesus and their group.

Once, Jesus and a large company of followers were headed south toward Jerusalem for Passover. None of the disciples realized Jesus was on His way to Jerusalem to die, in spite of His explicit predictions. They moved slowly, taking whole days here and there to minister to the crowds.

Jesus chose to travel through Samaria. There were other available routes, but Jesus had a reason for His choice. It was a bold, attention-getting move, a deliberate flouting of Jewish prejudices and standards. Many times before in His ministry, Jesus had ignored traditional Jewish taboos against contact with non-Jews. His willingness to cross the lines of exclusion warmed the hearts of the Samaritans. They told and embellished accounts of Jesus' friendship with their people. He had healed their citizens. He had eaten with them and even stayed overnight in their towns. Of all the rabbis in the world, Jesus was the one most welcome in Samaria.

Toward evening Jesus and his entourage approached a village where they planned to stay the night. But to the consternation of Jesus' entire party, the village elders turned them away. "Ordinarily," they said, "you'd be quite welcome here, but since you're on your way to Jerusalem, we don't think it proper for us to entertain you in our village."

John and his brother were outraged! Jesus' public kindnesses to Samaritans had cost him plenty in popular opinion in Judea. How dare these people do this? The brothers turned to Jesus, sputtering. "Master, do you want us to call fire down from heaven like Elijah did and burn them up?"

Jesus was not impressed. "You men don't realize what kind of spirit is operating in you when you talk like that," He said. "It certainly is not my Spirit. I did not come to destroy men but to save them." Luke 9:51-54, paraphrase.

John had thought he was doing Jesus a favor in offering to defend His honor. Of all people, these Samaritans owed Him better.

With this background, imagine what must have gone through John's mind on Thursday night. When the mob seized Jesus, he took off just like the rest of the disciples. But he didn't run far. And as the mob headed back into Jerusalem, John followed. The mob went straight to the high priest's palace. John had some connections in the high priest's household and was admitted into the courtyard without question. A little later he went out and found Peter and brought him in too.

The next twelve hours were the most horrific, the most difficult period of John's life. He listened to the bizarre accusations against Jesus. He saw his friend slapped around, mocked, abused, and beaten. And finally he saw Jesus nailed to the cross.

How many times must John have longed for power to set things right? How he wished that he and Peter had a small army at their command. But they didn't. They were helpless.

All John could do was watch. And what he saw transformed him.

John had seen Jesus prostrate the entire mob in Gethsemane, just before allowing them to seize Him. John knew that Jesus could at any moment overwhelm His tormentors and set Himself free. But Jesus accepted the insults and the physical abuse. And as He was stabbed with the pain of being nailed to the cross, John heard instead of a prayer for vengeance, the words, "Father, forgive them for they do not know what they're doing."

As John stood there on Golgotha, he witnessed the ultimate sermon about how we should respond to impiety, godlessness, blasphemy, and insult. Jesus absorbed the loss and prayed for His tormentors.

In later years, John, the erstwhile Son of Thunder, went on to write the gospel of love and the letter that includes these words:

> Whoever loves his brother lives in the light . . . But whoever hates his brother is in the darkness and walks around in the darkness; he does not know where he is going, because the darkness has blinded him.
>
> If anyone says, "I love God," yet hates his brother, he is a liar. For anyone who does not love his brother, whom he has seen, cannot love God, whom he has not seen. And he has given us this command: Whoever loves God must also love his brother.
>
> Dear children, let us not love with words or tongue but with actions and in truth (1 John 2:10, 11; 4:20, 21; 3:18).

John passed his graduate course in dealing with insults and provocations. God wants us to do the same.

When someone defames our church, it is tempting for us to indulge feelings similar to those that stirred John when his Master was insulted. We are outraged. We want to see the offender punished.

Perhaps the American equivalent of calling fire down from heaven is calling a lawyer.

Often our outrage is not really provoked by offenses against Jesus but by affronts to our own sense of dignity. We are not thanked for our hard work. We are not asked to continue in a position in which we have given superlative service. We are tempted to nurse bitter indignation. We wish stern justice against those who have slighted us.

Perhaps at work, someone who owes us favors, someone we have gone out of our way to help, participates in ousting us or blocking our promotion. We long for revenge. Jesus warns us: *Be careful. You do not realize what spirit is motivating you. It certainly isn't My Spirit.*

We have to be careful when we as Christians get into battles over our rights. When you hear of something outrageous that the ACLU has done in attempting to suppress the public expression of Christianity, be careful not to copy the spirit of James and John, the sons of thunder. Make sure you operate in the spirit of Jesus. What should you do when you hear of a school principal who is giving Christian students or teachers a rough time because of their faith? Instead of wishing that principal disaster, pray that God will use the confrontation to begin winning the heart of that principal.

When a political organization achieves a success that you see as threatening, or perhaps fulfilling prophecy, instead of calling them "the image to the Beast" or blasting them as Ayatollahs, respond to them as Jesus would.

When John wanted to call down fire from heaven on that village in Samaria, he was expressing a normal human desire for vengeance. When someone offends us, we feel there ought to be some kind of punishment. And when someone offends or insults our Jesus, our church, our faith, our natural instincts say the person ought to be punished.

And our instinct is not entirely wrong. Some day those who despise Jesus will have to face the judgment. The book of Revelation gives a terrifying picture of what it will be like to confront Jesus not as Saviour but as Judge.

> Then the kings of the earth, the princes, the generals, the rich, the mighty, and every slave and every free man hid in caves and among the rocks of the mountains. They called to the mountains and the rocks, "Fall on us and hide us from the face of him who sits on the throne and from the wrath of the Lamb! For the great day of their wrath has come, and who can stand?" (Revelation 6:15).

If your heart is broken because the honor of Jesus has been dragged in the dirt, remember it won't always be so. Those who despise Him, those who mock Him and refuse to repent will some day have a terrifying encounter.

But friend, it is not your job or mine to initiate that vengeance. Jesus plainly commanded us to love even our enemies and leave all vengeance to God.

John was ready to annihilate that Samaritan village when they slighted Jesus. Jesus on the other hand, extended forgiveness to people who not only insulted Him, but nailed Him to the cross. The apostle Paul wrote, "Be kind and compassionate to one another, forgiving each other, just as in Christ God forgave you. Be imitators of God, therefore, as dearly loved children" (Ephesians 4:32; 5:1).

Forgiveness has astonishing power. Liam McCloskey was

once a member of the Irish National Liberation Army. David Hamilton was a member of a loyalist paramilitary organization. Because of their politics and religion, they were bitter enemies. Then they both landed in jail. There, through the ministry of Prison Fellowship, they met Christ. They learned to forgive. As a result of their reconciliation, these two former enemies began to minister together, traveling across Northern Ireland preaching the value of forgiveness.

God does not want Christians battling each other in the streets or in the courts. God is appalled when people who bear the name of Christ attack others because of their supposedly wrong beliefs. Whether it's Northern Ireland or southern Mexico or Bosnia, Los Angeles or Toronto, Vanuatu or Hawaii, God calls on Christians to model His love, not His vengeance.

What about in your city or in your home? Are there people who need to be punished? Are there people whom you despise? Are there people who have hurt you or insulted you? Will you act as the child of your Father in heaven and forgive? Will you allow the spirit of Christ to control you, to work through you?

On His last night with His disciples, the night before He was crucified, Jesus told them, "You are my friends if you do what I command you. . . . This is my command: Love each other. Love as I have loved."

Paul described one specific expression of this kind of love when he wrote, "Be kind and compassionate to one another, forgiving each other, just as in Christ God forgave you" (Ephesians 4:32).

The next time you're tempted to attack someone who is wrong, stand with John on Golgotha. If you're a church administrator, beware of using modern violence (lawyers and the courts) against "Samaritans" or other enemies. Let's have the courage to renounce the use of lawsuits against those who name the name of Christ but don't respect the authority of the church. If you're a church member, beware of using lawsuits to fix the church. Instead of going to court, if we see a brother in sin, let's "pray and God will give him life" (1 John 5:16).

Let's resolve never to repeat, in our own fashion, the shameful riots of Constantinople or the wars of the Balkans or the troubles of Northern Ireland. Let's stand with John on Golgotha and complete our education. Let's learn with John to leave the thunder of judgment to the Judge of All.

First Place:
John, Part Two

"You know that those who are regarded as rulers of the Gentiles lord it over them, and their high officials exercise authority over them. Not so with you. Instead, whoever wants to become great among you must be your servant, and whoever wants to be first must be slave of all" (Mark 10:42, 43).

In the ongoing maneuvering for top spots in Jesus' future court, enlisting Mrs. Zebedee was a real coup. Jesus knew her well. She traveled with Him and participated with other women in supporting the work of Jesus and the Twelve.

After a bit of small talk, she came right to the point. "Teacher, I've been watching these young men You have helping You. They're a fine bunch. But it just seems obvious to me that none of them is as loyal and capable as my boys, here." John and James blushed. "I wish You'd promise to give them the number one and number two positions when You organize Your court. Why, with them at Your side, You'd never have to worry about a thing. I've talked to Your mother, Mary, and she and I both agree that my boys would do a great job."

Talk about your typical Hollywood mom!

When she finished, there was a long pause. Finally, Jesus responded, "You don't realize what you are asking." Then turning to her sons he asked, "Can you drink the cup I am going to drink? Do you really think you'll be able to endure with Me everything that's ahead of us?"

"Yes, sir," they answered.

Jesus surveyed them with a grave, penetrating look. Neither the young men nor their mother had the slightest conception of the punishing ordeal just weeks ahead. Jesus' glance shook them, sobered them. Then He smiled. "Yes, men, you will endure with Me. But the honor you're asking isn't Mine to give. It will be assigned by My Father in heaven."

Jesus refused to give James and John any assurance of specific honor. He *did* promise they would endure. They would be kept faithful.

Christians are called to endure, to persevere. We aren't called to chase fame and recognition.

Endurance doesn't mean the same thing for every Christian. Take John's brother, James, for instance. His service was dramatic, famous, and brief. Within a few years of this conversation with Jesus, he courageously faced execution. He was immediately honored by the church as their first martyr. John, on the other hand, spent years, perhaps decades, playing second fiddle, as Peter's junior partner.

Today John is honored as man who was the closest friend of Jesus. His Gospel is seen as the very pinnacle of Christian spiritual insight. But he earned this honor through decades of humble service. By the time he had come to be regarded as the grand patriarch of the church, he had spent a lifetime earning the honor. A lifetime of faithful endurance.

Endurance. For some it means heroic courage in a crisis. For others it means steady, anonymous faithfulness.

We cannot know the challenges that lie between us and the kingdom—persecution, civil unrest, long years of strenuous, unnoticed service, abandonment by friends, loss of health, years with a difficult spouse or child. But we do know the Master. Our future is secure with Him.

Within a few weeks at most after the attempt by Mrs. Zebedee and her sons to nail down top slots in Jesus' future government, she and John stood on Golgotha watching Jesus die. They were not alone. Jesus' mother was there along with other women from Galilee.

Standing there, watching his Master's agony, John fought back tidal waves of guilt. If only he had stayed awake to pray last night when Jesus asked him to. And stuck with Him when the mob showed up. His mind replayed over and over the mistakes he had made in Jesus' service. He cringed at the memories of his stupidity and pigheadedness. He had asked for first place among the ministers of the new kingdom. Now he doubted whether he was fit for any place. He hadn't been such a great assistant; he had hardly been a friend at all.

Later that day, he made his way through the crowd to the crosses, taking Jesus' mother with him. Jesus' agony, Mary's grief, and his own broken heart left John feeling useless, worthless. But then Jesus spoke. He could hardly talk, but He managed to rasp out two sentences. "Woman, there is your son." Then looking straight at John, "There is your mother."

In that instant John's anxious pursuit of a secure place in Jesus' friendship was satisfied. Jesus needed him, leaned on him.

Jesus demonstrates His acceptance of our friendship by asking us to care for His family. We experience friendship with Jesus primarily by being friends with His friends. John experienced this in a special way with Peter. Peter was always out front. He was loud, confident, and outgoing. He needed the steadiness of John. And John was there for him. He stood with Peter when Peter preached. He seconded Peter when Peter worked miracles in Jesus' name. He went to jail with Peter. He took pleasure in being a friend to a friend of Jesus.

Is friendship with Jesus the all-consuming passion of your life? Then don't allow anything to interfere with that friendship. Make sure you actively cultivate that relationship, keeping in mind that cultivating friendship with God must include developing friendships with His friends.

Do you want to be great in the kingdom of God? You can be. While there's no point in arguing about who is the greatest, there is value in enduring as a Christian soldier. Because if you endure, you'll receive an eternal place in Jesus' circle of friends. Do you want to know Jesus and be known by Him more than anything else in life? You won't be disappointed. Jesus' aim is to be able to say to all of us what He said to John and the other disciples on Thursday night before He died, " 'I no longer call you servants, because a servant does not know his master's business. Instead I have called you friends' " (John 15:15).

Friendship with Jesus may mean a rugged apprenticeship. If so, consider it an honor. He does not waste His discipline on people with no potential. "Endure hardship as discipline; God is treating you as sons. For what son is not disciplined by his father?" (Hebrews 12:7).

Jesus knew John's defects before He called him, but He called him just the same and equipped him for a major role in the kingdom of God. God chose John to put his stamp on the Christian church. Long after the rest of the apostles had died, for decades, in fact, John continued shaping the church through his preaching and personal influence. Jesus knew John's weaknesses. He knew his defects, but He also knew that John had learned the lessons of the cross. Jesus trusted John.

Jesus knows about your bad temper too. And your unbridled

ambition, your laziness, your incompetencies, your bad habits. Still He has chosen you. As He did with John, He will challenge you and correct you, but He needs you. He wants you to be His friend. He wants you to aim for first place in His kingdom of service.

The incontrovertible proof that Jesus has called you to be His friend is not your status in the church. Ordination is no proof of friendship with Jesus; lack of ordination is no evidence of distance from Christ's inner circle.

The proof of your call to friendship with Jesus, of your call to ministry, is the way Jesus leans on you to take care of His mother, father, brother, or sister. Maybe that means committing yourself to play ball regularly with the ten-year-old son of the single mother next door—or take him canoeing or take him with you when you go to your mother's house to fix a leaking faucet. Maybe Jesus is asking you to dig deeper into your income every month for some dollars to help a student stay in church school. Maybe he needs you to collaborate with your friends in writing anonymous, encouraging notes weekly for two months to a discouraged pastor. Jesus calls some of us to adopt and regularly visit an elderly neighbor or church member.

But above all, your friendship with Jesus will express itself in the way you treat your own mother or father, son or daughter, husband or wife. Jesus asks you to love Him by loving the people in your own household. Your mother may not have been perfect, but God calls you to love her anyway. And by love I do not mean merely some sentimental feeling; I mean deliberate actions that benefit your parents. Do it not because they deserve it but because you are a friend of Jesus, and He asks you to. Do it for Jesus.

I have friends who are keenly interested in theology. They enjoy debating the fine points of various issues by the hour. Some of them have very strong opinions about the precise definition of genuine Christianity, about the "pure gospel." But sometimes I wonder if a lot of what it means to be a Christian is simply showing up for work, doing what needs to be done. Working the night shift. Waiting on customers. Being faithful in your marriage when it's difficult. Going home to the spouse and kids when you'd rather not. Showing up at church two hours early to shovel the snow. At the very core of life as a Christian is showing ordinary kindness to those who need it most.

For the first two or three years of his association with Jesus, John constantly dreamed of winning first place in the court of the Messiah. He participated with the rest of the Twelve in their debates over who had the strongest claim to preeminence. And on Golgotha, Friday afternoon, Jesus indicated that John had won the contest.

But when John got the signal he had won, no one recognized the award. The proof of John's greatness in the eyes of Jesus was Jesus' request for him to take care of Mary, His mother.

It's no different in the church today. Often Jesus' special friends are not those with the obvious honors: church offices and titles and formal authority, academic credentials or popular acclaim as speakers. In the church, we are constantly fooled by our own traditions. The greatest among us is the servant, the one who cleans up after potluck, the ones willing to teach children's Sabbath School year after year, the one who seldom comes to church because she's at home taking care of a special-needs child or disabled spouse.

Jesus is looking for friends. He's looking for people who want to be great, who are willing to serve. He's looking for you.

İt İs Finished!

When he had received the drink, Jesus said, "It is finished." With that, he bowed his head and gave up his spirit (John 19:30).

For three and a half years Jesus worked nonstop. Sometimes He spent the entire night in prayer. Often He got up well before dawn to pray. He skipped meals so frequently His mother enlisted His brothers to help her force Him to take a break. She wanted Him to come home and get some rest and regular meals.

Jesus defended His busyness. When challenged about His activity on Sabbath, He replied: " 'My Father is always working, and I too must work' " (John 5:17, TEV). When questioned about His neglect of eating, He answered, " 'My food . . . is to do the will of him who sent me and to finish his work' " (John 4:34, NIV).

For three and a half years Jesus stopped for nothing and for no one. Then, hanging on the cross, He declared, "It is finished." Almost immediately He died. He was buried in a borrowed tomb and rested for an entire Sabbath day.

Throughout His ministry, Jesus pursued two inseparable goals: to show people what God was really like and to save people.

People desperately needed to see what God was really like. Life was hard for most folk, and they believed the harshness and fickleness of life reflected the personality of God. They imagined God as a distant, severe, hard-to-please dictator. Any favors you received you had to earn. Trouble and pain were proof that God was annoyed.

Jesus' mission was to fulfill the ancient prophecy:

> The people living in darkness have seen a great light; on those living in the land of the shadow of death a light has dawned. (Matthew 4:16).

Jesus was that great light. His ministry was a direct attack on darkness. He melted His way through the cold darkness of misunderstanding and gave people a new view, the real view, of God. The apostle John wrote,

> For the law was given through Moses, but grace and truth came through Jesus Christ. No one has seen God at any time. The only begotten Son, who is in the bosom of the Father, He has declared Him (John 1:17, 18, NKJV).

Matthew called Jesus Immanuel, which means "God with us." According to Paul, Jesus was the "visible likeness of the invisible God." Jesus Himself said, "Whoever has seen me has seen the Father" (Matthew 1:23; Colossians 1:15 TEV; John 14:9 TEV).

Coupled with His mission to make God known was Jesus' drive to save humanity. He felt great compassion for the common people in the harassment and helplessness of their lives.

They were like sheep without a shepherd, directionless and defenseless (Matthew 9:35, 36). Before Jesus was born, an angel told His stepfather, Joseph, "You shall call His name Jesus, for He will save His people from their sins" (Matthew 1:21, NKJV). Jesus Himself said He came " 'to seek and to save that which was the lost,' " not " 'to destroy men's lives but to save them' " (Luke 19:10; 9:56, NKJV).

Saving sinners was more important to Jesus than food or water or sleep or life itself. From the very beginning, an integral part of His mission as Saviour was the plan for Him to exchange places with people held hostage by sin. He would "give up his life as a ransom for many" (Matthew 20:28, NEB). Jesus came to provide real life, life in all its fullness, and He was under no illusions about the cost of His mission. It would cost His life. He gave it gladly and without compulsion (John 10:10-11, 15-18).

Jesus came to provide for our salvation. He came to make God known. He worked indefatigably until He accomplished those objectives. Then He declared His work finished, and, He rested. When He rose on Sunday, He did not resume the work He had been doing. It needed no additional attention; it was finished. After His ascension, Jesus began a totally new ministry in heaven.

The Friday of His crucifixion was not the first time the Son of God made a dramatic finish and rested. Jesus' first recorded rest came long before He took on a human nature. As the Son of God, Jesus was the member of the Godhead most directly responsible for the creation of this earth and its inhabitants. According to the apostle John, Jesus was the one "through whom all things were made."

Over a period of six days, Jesus created a perfect habitat for the first humans. It was complete with animals and plants. As the climax of His creative activity, on Friday afternoon He formed and gave life to Adam and Eve. But that was not the end of the week. Jesus, the Creator, completed the week by resting.

> By the seventh day God had finished the work he had been doing; so on the seventh day he rested from all his work. And God blessed the seventh day and made it holy, because on it he rested from all the work of creating that he had done (Genesis 2:2,3, NIV).

Since God does not get tired, we can draw two rather firm conclusions from His resting. First, He rested because He was satisfied with His creation. He was finished. There was no more to be done. The habitat for His children was perfect; His children were perfect. God was perfectly satisfied with everything He had made. Second, by His rest, He created an invitation for His children to stop their work and enjoy communion with Him.

On that very first Sabbath, humanity tasted something of the character of God. God invited them to rest, not because they had earned a rest or because they needed rest. (After all, they had been created, at most, a few hours before Sabbath began.) God invited them to rest because He wanted them to commune *with Him.* The first Sabbath was a powerful statement to men and women of their place in the affections of God.

On the Friday of His crucifixion, when Jesus declared "It is finished," He concluded a ministry paralleling creation. He had created a new reality by His perfect life and teachings and His willing sacrifice of Himself on the cross.

Jesus constructed a perfect life, which He could offer us in exchange for our own records of failure, rebellion, and sin. Jesus, alone of all humans, chose to be born. His life was His own in a way that is true of no other person. And He freely chose to offer that life to us as a gift. His entire life was a death march, but a death march with a purpose. He took our place in the march toward damnation. He drew all the fury of the enemy to Himself so we might escape unharmed. He gave His life as a ransom.

All sorts of people opposed Jesus' work—Pharisees, Sadducees, Herodians. The devil did his worst to hinder Jesus. Even Jesus' friends tried to interfere with His mission. Peter tried to talk Him out of dying. His mother, Mary, tried to control Him a few times. But nothing stopped Jesus—not hunger, not sleepiness, not opposition, not mistaken friendship, not indifference nor even human sinfulness and perversity. Jesus could not be stopped until He announced "It is finished." Just as He did not stop creating until everything was complete, so He did not stop working on revealing the Father and establishing our salvation until He was satisfied it was complete.

By the time He died, Jesus had so fully revealed God the Father that if you knew Jesus, you knew God (John 14:9). He had so strongly guaranteed salvation that He could say to the thief on the cross, "I can assure you, right now, you will be with me in Paradise" (Luke 23:43, paraphrase). He had so thoroughly counteracted the baleful effects of Adam's sin that Paul could write, "For as in Adam all die, so in Christ all will be made alive" (1 Corinthians 15:22). Everything that we lost through Adam (without our choice) has been restored in Christ.

When Jesus finally stopped on that Friday afternoon, He had done everything that needed to be done to provide salvation for you. "It is finished" is Jesus' promise to you. All is ready. Heaven is waiting for you to say Yes.

THE LOSER:
CAIAPHAS

"You know nothing at all! You do not realize that it
is better for you that one man die for the people than
that the whole nation perish (John 11:49, 50).

Caiaphas had it made. He came from a wealthy family. He
had married well. His wife was the daughter of Annas, one of
the most powerful persons in Jewish society at that time. Within
the past year he had reached the very pinnacle of Jewish greatness: High Priest of the temple in Jerusalem.

As high priest, he presided over the Sanhedrin. The sev-
enty-one member Sanhedrin served as supreme court and leg-
islature both politically and religiously for the country of Judea.
And it was the supreme religious body for international Judaism. Its influence reached all the way to Spain in the west, to
Egypt in the south, to the imperial capital, Rome, and perhaps as far as India in the east.

Other than the emperor of Rome, probably no one in all
the ancient Middle East had as far ranging an influence as the
high priest of Jerusalem.

Working with Caiaphas in the Sanhedrin were some of the

finest minds in Judaism, scholars versed in the Sacred Scriptures and the extensive body of rabbinic commentary. They were religious men and family men. Caiaphas was a member of the liberal group called the Sadducees.

If Caiaphas had one passion other than his own personal career advancement, it was the honor of his nation and the temple. He would allow nothing to threaten the independence of Israel or to diminish the honor of the temple. He was prepared to sacrifice anything—people, principle, integrity—to save the institutions of his people: the temple, the priesthood, and the scant measure of political autonomy allowed them by the Romans.

Caiaphas took great delight in the sense of power and importance that came from serving as high priest. There was, however, one disturbance, one irritation, that had been present from the very beginning of Caiaphas's tenure as high priest. And that was Jesus of Nazareth.

Jesus had been a problem ever since He began public ministry. When reports reached the Sanhedrin that John the Baptist had announced the appearance of the Messiah, Caiaphas groaned. *Not another one! It seemed that every year some new Messianic frenzy seized the people. The Baptist had been disruptive enough already; now this!*

Not long afterward, a mysterious Man had run all the cattle dealers and money-changers out of the temple courtyard. It was preposterous! The Man had been unarmed, unless you call a bit of rope a weapon. He had no entourage to speak of. He simply ordered the merchants to leave then strode among them, shooing them out like a farmer scattering crows from a garden. Upon investigation, it turned out that this was John the Baptist's Messiah.

Right then Caiaphas knew they had a problem. He was not yet high priest, but he was part of the inner circle in the

Sanhedrin. He tried to warn them that decisive action was needed immediately. This Man was dangerous. He had enormous charisma, and He understood nothing of the importance of compromise nor of institutional stability.

The disturbing reports continued to come in over the next three and a half years. Fortunately, the Nazarene didn't settle in Jerusalem. Instead, He spent most of His time up north in Galilee among the peasants. But accounts reaching Jerusalem were unbelievable. He supposedly fed more than five thousand people one afternoon, starting with nothing more than a lad's lunch. Credible spies reported His curing lepers and people with congenital deformities. He healed everything—all kinds of diseases, epilepsy, demon possession. It seemed nothing was too hard for the Man.

In addition to His powers as a healer and as a master over evil spirits, He was an irresistible preacher. Every time someone wanted to argue, He would draw them into a story that made His point without argument, leaving the would-be debater sheepish and frustrated. The Man refused to be drawn into detailed analyses of current controversies, instead He—well, He told stories. How do you debate a man who tells stories? The Pharisees tried; members of Caiaphas's own Sadducee party tried; even the Herodians tried. It was no use. Instead, the whole country was retelling stories that Jesus first used to rebuff His opponents.

Caiaphas couldn't understand Jesus. Usually preachers like Him tried to impress the crowds by lambasting corruption in the priesthood. Jesus obviously had enough information to keep scandal hounds busy for a long time. And Jesus' audiences were packed with malcontents, just the sort of people who could be inflamed with fresh news of wickedness in high places.

But while He was blunt in His condemnation of sin and in

His advocacy of what He called "the truth," Jesus seemed to go out of His way to avoid attacking the leadership of the nation.

Caiaphas didn't know how to get at Jesus. How do you fight someone who can't be provoked? Jesus consorted with all sorts of sinners, but Caiaphas's agents could find not even a whiff of scandal.

Jesus was drawing huge crowds. His preaching was unsettling the people. There was talk among the common people of seizing Him and making Him king by force. His emphasis on purity and service provoked profound dissatisfaction among the people with the current state of the priesthood. Caiaphas feared the day was not too distant when he would be unable to challenge Jesus; the Preacher's popular support would be too strong.

Then Caiaphas was made high priest. Now he had the authority to really move against Jesus. Still, he had to win the consent of the rest of the council for an arrest. And that seemed almost impossible to do.

Finally, one day, exasperated at the hand wringing and whining of other council members as they discussed the problem of Jesus, Caiaphas blurted out, "You men know nothing at all! Don't you know that it is expedient for us, that one man should die rather than the whole nation?" It was the turning point. It seemed to cut through the hesitancy of the council. From then on there was a growing consensus to eliminate Jesus as quickly and cleanly as possible.

About the same time, one of Jesus' inner circle had offered to provide information on Jesus' movements, and he didn't demand too much money for his services. It was just the break they needed. Clearly, God was helping them. God had simply been waiting for them to take decisive action.

A week later, Jesus was under arrest in Caiaphas's mansion. Caiaphas summoned the council for a quick trial. But it did *not* go as smoothly as he expected. Except for Nicodemus and Joseph, he had been sure the members either agreed with him or would keep quiet. Caiaphas had taken care of Nicodemus and Joseph by having them conveniently overlooked when members were notified of the meeting. But still too many inconvenient questions were asked by other members of the council. The witnesses were a disaster, contradicting each other or giving useless information.

Caiaphas began to wonder if Jesus was the cat and he was the mouse.

The priest shook his head, disgusted with himself for allowing such cowardice into his head, but Jesus' presence seemed to unnerve witnesses and council alike. Finally two witnesses agreed they had heard Jesus say something like "I am going to destroy the temple and rebuild it in three days." It was a piece of nonsense as they reported it, but it gave Caiaphas something to work with. He challenged Jesus to defend Himself, to answer the charges. He desperately wanted to draw Jesus into the argument of the trial. Instead, Jesus stood there silent, like a judge waiting for the hubbub to die down before pronouncing sentence. Caiaphas ground his teeth. Why didn't this man fight?

Losing all control, Caiaphas shouted, "In the name of the living God, I adjure you. Tell us who you are! Are you the Messiah, the Son of God?"

Jesus fixed Caiaphas with His eyes. "Yes, it is as you say." Then looking around the room, He continued. "But I tell all of you, in the future you will see the Son of Man sitting at the right hand of the Almighty and coming on the clouds of heaven."

For a split second, Caiaphas was frozen with terror. Jesus' unmoving posture and steady eyes drove the words straight through the high priest. Time stopped. The entire assembly held its breath. Would Caiaphas bend? Would the council be persuaded?

Suddenly Caiaphas leapt from his seat. Grabbing the lapels of his robe, he ripped it down the front, shouting, "He has spoken blasphemy! What do we need witnesses for? You heard him. What do you say?"

His bold theatrics saved him. The council shouted back. "He is worthy of death."

Through Moses, God had forbidden high priests to tear their robes, even in reaction against blasphemy. In fact, God prescribed the death penalty for any high priest who tore his robes. But dramatic action had been needed to offset the power of the Man Jesus Christ. The very future of the nation hung in the balance. Caiaphas was certain that if he didn't stop Jesus now, there might well be a popular insurrection. And if that ever happened, the Romans would send in troops, dismiss the Sanhedrin, and occupy the temple mount. Everything would be lost. Jesus had to be stopped whatever it cost.

Caiaphas sank back in his chair. He motioned with his hand to the guards attending Jesus. They yanked Him around and shoved Him ahead of them toward the back of the room where they were joined by others in abusing Him.

For Caiaphas, there was still work to do. At daybreak he reconvened the council to meet the legal requirement that trials be held during the day. After rubber-stamping their earlier decision, the council, at Caiaphas's urging, marched en masse with Jesus to the Roman governor's palace.

Pilate, the governor, was more obstinate than usual as they pressed him to ratify their death sentence. But finally he ordered the execution.

Caiaphas and other priests followed Jesus out to Golgotha. They saw Him nailed and lifted against the sky. Caiaphas feared He would come down. He recalled too vividly the stories of Jesus' incredible powers. Jesus' eyes burned in his mind. Jesus' words reechoed through his memory: "You will see the Son of Man sitting at the right hand of the Almighty and coming in the clouds."

Jesus of Nazareth had spoken as a judge. And the high priest could not shake the condemnation from his mind. He tried to forget the words by joining the taunts of the mob. "If God likes you so much, why doesn't He save you?" He shouted. "You saved others; save yourself. Maybe then, even I will become a believer." Caiaphas forced a strained and nervous laugh.

But Jesus didn't save Himself. Through the afternoon He slowly died. News of Jesus' death lifted a huge weight from Caiaphas's shoulders. Finally they were rid of Him. Caiaphas had saved the temple, the nation, and his own career. He was free.

It was too bad the Man had to die but better this one man than the entire nation face extinction.

But the first rush of relief Caiaphas experienced when Jesus died quickly evaporated. He began remembering with growing dread statements Jesus had made about rising again. What if Jesus' disciples made off with Jesus' body and claimed He had risen? Even though he was breaking all conservative norms of Sabbath keeping, the very next day, Sabbath, the high priest went to see the Roman governor.

"Sir," Caiaphas said to Pilate. "We remember that this deceiver predicted while he was still alive that he would die and then rise again after three days. If his disciples were to take his body and hide it and then spread the story that he had been resurrected . . . I don't think I need to say more." He gave Pilate a knowing smile.

"Go on." Pilate agreed. "You may have a guard detail. Make the tomb as secure as you can." (Was there here already in Pilate's words, "as secure as you can," a note of uneasiness, a doubt whether they or any human force could really contain Jesus?)

The posting of a guard of professional, veteran troops at the grave and the sealing of the grave with an official seal of the Roman procurator made Caiaphas feel better. It would make sure that everyone knew Jesus was really dead, no matter what story the disciples might try to invent. Of course, what Caiaphas could not know is that his arrangements for securing the tomb would become the strongest proof that the disciples were telling the truth when they announced to the world: He is risen.

There is no exaggerating the kindness and gentleness of Jesus. But it is possible to distort them. Jesus is not just tact and courtesy and gentleness. Jesus is rugged and strong. He stands for righteousness and justice. And those who persist in opposing Him find that He is unbreakable.

Erich Honecker, the last real president of Communist East Germany, died Sunday, May 29, 1994, a bitter, broken man. He had poured his entire life into a lost cause.

He had imprisoned and killed his fellow East Germans in a relentless pursuit of a pure Stalinist state. What happened? He lost to Christ.

His regime was toppled by demonstrations in the streets led largely by Christian pastors.

How did the people he had ruled feel when he died? "At this point," one man said, "I couldn't care less about Honecker, and I'm sure the same goes for most East Germans." The final irony was that after he was driven from power and was dying of a terminal illness no one would take care of him. No hospital wanted him in one of their beds; the administrators didn't dare allow their institution to be associated with the hated man in any way. Finally, a couple came to his rescue, a Christian pastor and his wife. They took Erich Honecker into their own home and nursed him till he died.

Honecker devoted his life to fighting Christ. He lost. Jesus won.

For seventy years the leaders of the Soviet Union did everything they could to stamp out belief in Jesus Christ. Now they are inviting Christians to come into their schools, their military academies, and even into the offices of the police and teach people about God.

It is a hopeless cause to fight Christ. In the end you lose.

On the other hand, if you will ally yourself with Jesus, His victory will be yours. Your life will not be wasted. Your failures will all be temporary.

The Bible's last snapshot of Caiaphas is in Acts, chapter 5. Jesus has returned to heaven and sent the Holy Spirit to His people. In the power of the Spirit, Peter and the other apostles have been preaching with amazing effect. Thousands of people have publicly been baptized in the name of Jesus of Nazareth. Several thousand even of the priesthood have become believers!

Caiaphas makes his last assault on Jesus of Nazareth—this time in the person of his disciples. The high priest has the apostles arrested and brought before the council. But when he attempts to rebuke them for their witnessing, they indict him. "You killed Jesus!" they declare, "But God raised Him from the dead and has exalted Him to His own right hand as Prince and Saviour." Caiaphas did not hear the rest of their speech; instead, Christ's words rang in his mind, "You will see the Son of Man sitting at the right hand of the Almighty and coming in the clouds." In his mind's eye, he felt again the Judge's steady gaze.

Caiaphas tried to persuade the council to have the disciples executed. But the council refused. Caiaphas was defeated. As sort of a last gasp, he got the council to approve having the Christians flogged. But it accomplished nothing.

Caiaphas had crucified the Nazarene. But he could not keep Him dead. He had tried to quash public interest in Jesus, but the city was filling with impressionable devotees. Jesus had won.

The apostles went home praising God that they had been counted worthy to suffer for the Name of Jesus. Caiaphas went home a broken man.

Jesus spoke of Himself when He said: " 'He who falls on this stone will be broken to pieces, but he on whom it falls will be crushed' " (Matthew 21:44).

Jesus will triumph. That much is absolutely certain. You may come to Him now with your brokenness and be assured that He will heal you and eventually give you a home in His kingdom. Or you may reject Him and fight Him and finally be crushed by His victory. The choice is yours.

Into Your Hands

Jesus knew the thrill of popularity, no doubt about that. He often had been surrounded by crowds of thousands. So many people wanted His attention that He didn't have time even to eat. Thousands hung on His every word. Other thousands wanted to touch Him or be touched by Him. At times when He preached beside Lake Galilee, He had to have a boat ready in case the crowd actually pushed Him into the water in their eagerness.

After He resurrected the son of a widow from the little village of Nain, the people "were filled with awe and praised God. 'A great prophet has appeared among us,' they said" (Luke 7:16). The common people delighted in His frequent arguments with scholars and religious dignitaries. They cheered when He confounded these representatives of the establishment. Popular enthusiasm for Jesus was so intense that the nation's elite lived in constant dread of a popular uprising to put Him on the throne.

Jesus knew the crowds were putty in His hands—at least as far as political or mass action was concerned. He could have manipulated them in almost any direction He wished. And

He cared deeply for these ordinary people. Their needs touched Him. He spent Himself for them without reserve. But Jesus did not play to the crowd—not to their applause or their needs. The crowd did not control Him. In fact, Jesus did not hesitate to alienate His popular support when keeping that support would have required soft-pedaling His message. Jesus played to God.

In contrast to His immense popularity among the masses, Jesus faced fierce, relentless opposition from the ruling elite. They accused Him of being in league with the devil, accused Him of blasphemy and treason. They hounded Him with spies and clever questioners looking for something they could pin on Him in court.

Jesus scandalized the religious and political leaders by fraternizing with tax collectors and other "sinners," as they called them, people from the moral bottom of society.

But just as He could not be manipulated by the acclaim of the masses, neither could He be controlled by official opposition. Once, after He had spoken forcefully against using religious obligations as a dodge to avoid caring for one's extended family, His disciples asked Him, "Don't you know that the Pharisees were offended when they heard this?"

Did Jesus backpedal or soften His message? No, He pressed even harder. " 'Every plant that my heavenly Father has not planted will be pulled up by the roots. Leave them; they are blind guides. If a blind man leads a blind man, both will fall into a pit' " (Matthew 15:13,14).

Jesus challenged the religious establishment by socializing with the wrong people, by publicly violating historic Sabbath taboos, by neglecting miscellaneous traditions, and, on rare occasions, by publicly denouncing the hypocrisy or unbelief of religious leaders. But He did not define His ministry by opposition to the establishment or rebellion against ancient customs. He did not shape His ministry as a rebuttal of His detractors. Nor did He bend and compromise to try to blunt their opposition. Jesus simply did what was right. He spoke the truth no matter whom it pleased or offended. Jesus played to God.

A truly dramatic demonstration of this independence occurred on Jesus' last trip from Galilee to Jerusalem, the trip that ended with His crucifixion. Jesus passed through the city of Jericho in the Jordan Valley, a wealthy town on an important trade route. Because it was near the border and served as a customs collection point, it had a large cadre of tax collectors who worked for the Romans.

The chief tax collector in town was a well-to-do man named Zacchaeus. Learning that Jesus was coming into town, he joined the crowds in the streets vying for a glimpse of the Preacher. Zacchaeus was short and could not see over the heads of the crowd; because of the hatred he had earned as tax collector, he dared not try to press his way through to the front of the crowd. Strange and unhealthy things could happen to a little, hated tax collector deep in the heart of an excitable crowd.

Running ahead of the procession, he climbed a tree that branched out over the street. He and the entire city were astounded when the famous Preacher stopped under the tree, looked up, and invited Himself to dinner!

Zacchaeus was thrilled; the rest of the crowd was disgusted. Tax collectors in Israel had lower social status than drug pushers do in today's communities. They were despised and loathed as traitors who had sold out to an oppressive invader. Since Israel was a theocracy, collaboration with a foreign occupying army was not only treason; it was akin to idolatry. But Jesus seemed oblivious to public opinion, or perhaps He was deliberately flouting it. He was intent on connecting with one man and making a friend of him. Jesus succeeded. When Jesus left town, Zacchaeus was a changed man.

This dinner in the home of a chief tax collector, a chief of sinners, was a fitting capstone of Jesus' social ministry. He constantly looked for the lowliest, the neediest, the most reprobate to serve. Jesus welcomed into His circle of friends people like Mary Magdalene and Matthew, whom we have met elsewhere in this book. He touched lepers, who were legally untouchable, and ate and slept in the homes of Samaritans, who were considered beyond the reach of God's mercy. Repeatedly in the Gospels we encounter the complaint of society's guardians of morality: This man welcomes sinners and eats with them. He is a friend of tax collectors and sinners (Luke 15:2; Matthew 11:19).

Jesus' dinner at the home of Zacchaeus fits His pattern of embracing the lowly, of refusing to cater to the prejudices of the elite. But a day or two later Jesus went to another dinner that demonstrated His independence as well from the prejudices of the hoi polloi. Jesus went to eat in the home of Simon the Pharisee.

Jesus was as interested in the well-being of Pharisees and priests as He was in that of tax collectors and prostitutes. His mission was to seek and save the lost. And that included all mankind, not just selected social or religious groups. During the last week of His life, Jesus blasted the religious leaders for their obstinate persistence in hypocrisy, for their spiritual bankruptcy that damaged not only themselves but the world around them. Then, after having spoken more sternly than at any other time in His ministry, Jesus cried out,

> O Jerusalem, Jerusalem, you who kill the prophets and stone those sent to you, how often I have longed to gather your children together, as a hen gathers her chicks under her wings, but your were not willing (Matthew 23:37).

The entire city, the entire people—leaders and nobodies, saints and reprobates, respectable and despicable. Jesus wanted to gather them into the joy and security of His kingdom. That was the reason He had come to earth. That was the mission assigned Him by His heavenly Father. And nothing could turn Him from it.

When Jesus was crucified, He ended His life as He had lived it—focused on God. On the cross He prayed for His tormentors. He arranged for someone to care for His mother. He offered comfort and assurance of salvation to a dying thief. He cried out in agony as He felt the withdrawal of His Father's presence. But as death closed on Him, He cried out, " 'Father, into your hands I commit my spirit.' "

He had lived for God. Now He died for God. He entrusted Himself to God.

Jesus' final cry takes on special significance when we look at it as the climax to His experience on the cross. In Gethsemane Jesus had agonized over His mission on the cross, agony so intense that His body began to break down and He sweat blood. Then had come the arrest and His formal condemnation by the religious leaders of His people. He had been beaten then nailed to a cross. Then to cap it off, He endured the wrenching sense of separation from His Father.

Hope, which was His by right, was not His by experience. The future, which He had seen clearly and predicted—the chief priests will hand me over for crucifixion and on the third day I will rise—because of physical and emotional pain was now opaque and incredible. As happens to all humans, pain had shrunk the universe around Jesus until there was nothing but His overwhelming pain. But out of the crushing blackness He thrust His hand in hope toward God: " 'Father, into your hands I commit my spirit.' "

Jesus appeared God-forsaken. He was enduring the shame

and soul-bending pain of crucifixion. As far as He can tell from what He is experiencing, He is being utterly abandoned by God. God has let Him down.

But Jesus refuses to believe appearances. He rejects the testimony of His emotions and His immediate experience. He claims God's favor and attention in spite of what He feels. He entrusts Himself absolutely to God. "Father, into your hands I commit my spirit."

On the cross, Jesus felt utterly God-forsaken. Still He placed himself unreservedly in God's hands. You can do the same no matter how God-forsaken you feel. Place yourself in God's hands. Make Him responsible for your future and your well-being. You cannot be in better hands.

Once during Jesus' ministry, while He was "on vacation" near the town of Tyre, outside Israel, a Gentile woman approached Him begging for help for her demon-possessed daughter. Jesus pretended to ignore her then He explicitly declared she did not belong to the demographic group that was the target of His ministry. But this woman simply refused to accept the apparent rejection. She insisted on trusting Him. Call her a dog if you choose, but she would still insist on the crumbs that fell from the Master's table. He saluted her for her faith and gave her what she needed (Matthew 15:21-28).

In our own lives we sometimes project onto God the rejection we've experienced from other people. If a church leader or our parents rejected us, then surely God would have nothing to do with us. But since Jesus played to God, He was unresponsive to the attempts by His disciples to be "selective" in the people He befriended. Jesus had been sent to save sinners. His mission was to carry out the will of the Godhead, and God wanted not a single person lost (2 Peter 3:9). So we never have to wonder whether heaven will be open to our cry for help or for acceptance and new life.

When our emotions or sense of guilt insist that God cares nothing for us, we can choose to trust God anyway. We can give ourselves into His hands. We cry out like the father whose son was tormented by demons: " 'Lord, I believe; help my unbelief' " (Mark 9:24, NKJV). Or reach out in silent desperation like the woman who furtively touched Jesus' robe as He passed in the crowd, telling herself, " 'if I just touch his clothes, I will be healed' " (Mark 5:28). She was right. She was healed. And if you are hungry for righteousness, it's always safe to trust yourself to God. "For God did not send His Son into the world to condemn the world, but that the world might be saved through Him" (John 3:17, paraphrase). " 'He has filled the hungry with good things but has sent the rich away empty' " (Luke 1:53).

No matter what your emotions or other people tell you, God is eager for you to entrust yourself to Him. He will forgive your sins and work in you by His Holy Spirit to transform your character, and ultimately He will welcome you into His kingdom.

When you live with reference to God, you are liberated from preoccupation with external success and failure. At every point in your life you can confidently say with Jesus, "Father, into your hands I commit my spirit."

You cannot be in better hands.

This prayer changes the focus of our lives. Instead of being preoccupied with our performance, we focus our attention on the trustworthiness, the graciousness of God. When we spend too much time considering ourselves, we can be overcome with discouragement. We are not "good enough." But when we focus on God, we are filled with confidence and hope. Given the richness of His love, the enormity of His power, and the intensity of His affection, how could anyone be lost?

In this book, we have looked at the cross through many different eyes. We have listened to Jesus' cries from the cross through many different ears. We learn something different from every person, from each saying. But ultimately, God wants us to know Jesus for ourselves. And as we get acquainted with Jesus, we, in fact, come to know God.

If you have never done so before, I invite you right now to say to the Father, Son, and Holy Spirit, "Into your hands I commit my spirit." Give yourself to God right now and taste for yourself the joy, the freedom, the triumph that God gives those who commit themselves to Him.